Men-at-Arms • 556

Germany's French Allies 1941–1945

Massimiliano Afiero • Illustrated by Ramiro Bujeiro

Series editors: Martin Windrow & Nick Reynolds

OSPREY PUBLISHING
Bloomsbury Publishing Plc
Kemp House, Chawley Park, Cumnor Hill, Oxford OX2 9PH, UK
29 Earlsfort Terrace, Dublin 2, Ireland
1385 Broadway, 5th Floor, New York, NY 10018, USA
E-mail: info@ospreypublishing.com
www.ospreypublishing.com

OSPREY is a trademark of Osprey Publishing Ltd

First published in Great Britain in 2024

© Osprey Publishing Ltd, 2024

A catalogue record for this book is available from the British Library

ISBN: PB 9781472862983; eBook 9781472862990;
ePDF 9781472863003; XML 9781472862976

24 25 26 27 28   10 9 8 7 6 5 4 3 2 1

Editor: Martin Windrow
Map by the author
Index by Fionbar Lyons
Typeset by PDQ Digital Media Solutions, Bungay, UK
Printed in India by Replika Press Private Ltd

MIX
Paper from
responsible sources
FSC
www.fsc.org   FSC® C016779

Osprey Publishing supports the Woodland Trust, the UK's leading woodland conservation charity.

To find out more about our authors and books, visit
www.ospreypublishing.com. Here you will find extracts, author interviews, details of forthcoming events and the option to sign up for our newsletter.

Author's note and acknowledgements

To retrace the history of the French units in German service during World War II, I have referred mainly to archival documents and wartime publications, but also to published works on French volunteers in the Wehrmacht and Waffen-SS (see Bibliography). Most of the photos, unless otherwise specified, were obtained from the US National Archives, or from the private collections of the author and of Christopher Chatelet, René Chavez and Hugh Page Taylor. I take this opportunity to thank them and other friends and collaborators who have generously contributed to this new work, and in particular René Chavez and Christopher Chatelet.

As always, I also owe a particular debt to my illustrator, Ramiro Bujeiro, for his patient and thorough uniform research.

Editor's note

To avoid confusion, in the body text we *italicize* only French-language terms, not German.

In captions and plate commentaries, German names for e.g. items of uniform are also italicized.

LVF (German Army) ranks are abbreviated in either French or German, Waffen-SS ranks in German, and in both cases an approximate English equivalent abbreviation is included with first use.
In the text, place-names are given as they appear in German wartime sources, in sometimes debatable transcription from Russian Cyrillic.

TITLE PAGE
Photo from a wartime German book, illustrating a volunteer of III Btl / LVF in May 1942 during the unit's first anti-partisan deployment with 221. Sicherungs-Div in the Smolensk area. In hot weather and marshy terrain, he wears a Wehrmacht-issue mosquito-netting hood over his helmeted head (see Plate C2).

OPPOSITE
Unteroffizier (*caporal or caporal-chief*) of the *Légion des Volontaires Français* on the Eastern Front, 1941/42. Note the German Army-issue October 1941 sleeve shield surmounted by 'FRANCE' in white on a black strip – see Plate H2. (Photo from German wartime magazine '*Signal*')

GERMANY'S FRENCH ALLIES 1941–1945

OVERVIEW

On 10 May 1940 the German armed forces (Wehrmacht) opened their assault on Western Europe. By 4 June the Netherlands and Belgium had surrendered, and the British Expeditionary Force (BEF) had narrowly escaped back over the English Channel. France still had some 60 operational divisions, but on 14 June German troops entered Paris unopposed.

On the 16th the French premier, Paul Renault, handed over power to a group including the 84-year-old Marshal Philippe Pétain, a long-retired hero of World War I who enjoyed great popular prestige. On 17 June, Pétain broadcast that he had agreed to head a government which would seek an armistice with Germany, and this was duly signed on 22 June. Its major terms included the division of metropolitan France into two zones: the north, plus the whole Atlantic coast, fell under German military occupation, while the Unoccupied Zone in the centre and south would be governed directly by a regime headed by Pétain and based in the city of Vichy. The government of this 'French State' (whose *de facto* prime minister was a convinced collaborator, Pierre Laval) also retained authority over France's overseas colonies. In addition to the latters' garrisons of the *Troupes Coloniales* and *Armée d'Afrique*, Vichy was permitted a 100,000-strong 'Armistice Army' in the Unoccupied Zone.

A year later, in France as in some other occupied countries, Germany's invasion of the Soviet Union (USSR) on 22 June 1941 – which Goebbels' propaganda machine hailed as a 'crusade against Bolshevism' – attracted some popular support, and led to the formation of a French volunteer force to fight under Wehrmacht command on the Eastern Front. This *Légion des Volontaires Français* (LVF) was given the Wehrmacht designation Verstaerktes Französische Infanterie-Regiment 638 (638th French Reinforced Infantry Regiment), and reached the Moscow front in time for the terrible 1941/42 winter campaign. Rebuilt after suffering crippling losses in December 1941, thereafter it was long employed on security operations against partisan bands behind the front lines of Army Group Centre. In 1944 the LVF again saw punishing action against regular Red Army forces, before being transferred from the Deutsches Heer (German Army) into the Waffen-SS.

3

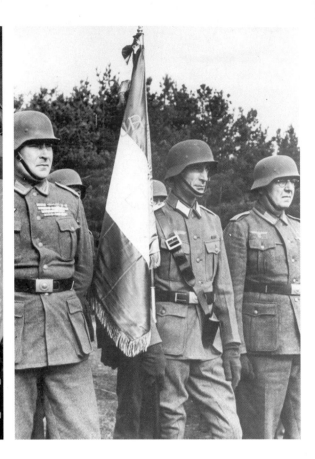

In mid-1942 the Vichy government attempted to create its own national force, the ***Légion Tricolore***, to subsume the LVF, whose complete absorption into the German Army was resented by French nationalists. On 12 July 1942 Joseph Darnand – head of the *Service d'Ordre Légionnaire* (SOL), the paramilitary arm of Vichy's political organization of ex-soldiers, the *Légion Française des Combattants* (LFC) – announced that the Tricolour Legion would fight alongside the Axis (and indeed boasted that it would wear French rather than German uniforms). Its creation was celebrated on 28 August 1942 at a ceremony held in Vichy in the presence of Otto Abetz, Germany's ambassador to France, but the Germans thereafter gave it neither encouragement nor military status. In November 1942 Anglo-American forces landed in French North Africa, and an almost immediate armistice there provoked the Axis occupation of the previously Unoccupied Zone of France. The Pétain regime's authority was ostensibly preserved, but the Armistice Army was disbanded, and so was the Tricolour Legion (although aspects of its infrastructure in France continued to serve the LVF). A small number of its personnel chose to join the ranks of the LVF in Russia.

During the Axis reinforcement of the Tunisian front, a plan to create a French voluntary corps to fight there – the ***Phalange Africaine*** ('African Phalanx') – was approved by Laval on 24 November 1942, and authorized by the Germans at the beginning of December as the Französische Freiwilligen Legion ('French Volunteer Legion'). Recruiting began in France, and a military mission flew to Tunisia to recruit locally. Training soon began, and by April 1943 a reinforced company had been formed. Commanded by Capt André Dupuis, this force was engaged from 9 to

27 April in the Medjez El-Bab sector against troops of the British 78th Inf Div, dissolving just before the Axis surrender in early May.

Since 1940, individual French volunteers had also enlisted in the **Waffen-SS**. However, it was only after the Axis occupation of the whole of France that Himmler proposed the creation of an entire French volunteer SS unit, and Laval authorized French citizens to enlist in the Waffen-SS with effect from 22 July 1943. Among the volunteers were many members of Darnand's *Milice Française* internal security militia, which had been formed on 5 January 1943. The volunteers were transported to Sennheim camp in Alsace for training, and on 18 August 1943 the order came for the formation of a Französisches SS-Freiwilligen-Grenadier-Regiment. ('Grenadier' was the purely honorary new title for most German infantrymen, ordered by Hitler on 2 November 1942.) On 22 January 1944 the French regiment received the new designation of SS-Frw-Gren-Rgt 57 (französische nr.1), which was subsequently enlarged into a Französische Frw-Sturmbrigade der SS. In July 1944 this sent a French battle group to the Carpathian front in Galicia; deployed with 18. SS-Frw-PzGren-Div 'Horst Wessel' against Soviet troops in the Sanok sector, it suffered very heavy losses in August.

In September 1944 the Germans decided to assemble all French volunteers enrolled in their military and paramilitary forces (the LVF, Kriegsmarine (German Navy), NSKK (National Socialist Motor Corps), the Organization Todt construction service, plus the French *Milice*) into a new Waffen-Grenadier-Brigade der SS 'Charlemagne', which would subsequently become (on paper, at least) the 33. W-Gren-Div

der SS 'Charlemagne' (französische nr.1). Its units were deployed in February 1945 on the Pomeranian front, where they were almost annihilated. The division was then officially reduced to a regiment, of which an assault battalion would take part in the last battles in the streets of Berlin.

LA LÉGION DES VOLONTAIRES FRANÇAIS

Creation

In the Occupied Zone, since 1940 the Germans had watchfully tolerated a number of mutually competitive far-right movements (the 'Paris Ultras'), which varied in their sizes and agendas. On 7 July 1941 the leaders of the main parties met at the Hotel Majestic in Paris to form a committee to discuss the creation of a French volunteer unit to fight on the Russian Front. The following day, Paris newspapers announced the formation of the *Légion des Volontaires Français contre le bolchevisme* (LVF). In Vichy France the recruitment of volunteers was entrusted to an Action Committee in Marseilles, organized by the fascist *Parti Populaire Français* (PPF). On 18 July the LVF central committee organized its first rally at the Paris *Vélodrome d'Hiver* (winter cycling stadium), which was attended by more than 10,000 people.

Actual enrolment of volunteers began with a ceremony on 27 August at the Borgnis-Desbordes barracks in Versailles. Almost 1,700 volunteers showed up on the first day, but of these only about 800 would manage to pass strict German medical examinations. The aspiring legionaries came from all backgrounds, united only in their anti-communism; many clung to their factional rivalries, particularly between the PPF, the *Mouvement Social Révolutionnaire* (MSR), and the *Rassemblement National Populaire* (RNP). As well as political extremists they included veterans, policemen, firefighters, postmen and ex-soldiers of the French Foreign Legion – but among them were also conservative aristocrats and, for instance, Jean, Count of Mayol de Lupé, a monsignor of the Vatican curia and friend of Pope Pius XII. At the end of the recruitment campaign only some 2,500 of 13,400 applicants had been accepted, and the formation of a two-battalion regiment was decided. Its first commander was the 60-year-old *Col* Roger Labonne, a professor of military history. On 3 September 1941, a regimental flag was presented to the legionaries during a solemn ceremony.

The following day the first contingent of 828 volunteers left for the Debica training ground in Poland. By early October the arrival of many others had brought total strength to 2,271 including 181 officers, plus a German liaison staff of 35 officers and NCOs. Since France was not officially at war with the Soviet Union, the volunteers of Verstaerktes Französische Infanterie-Regiment 638 (the 638th French Reinforced Inf Rgt) – like those from other countries – would wear German uniform and rank insignia, with a sleeve patch in national colours. A tricolour decal

On the Galician front in August 1944, W-Oberjunker Abel Chapy distinguished himself by his leadership during the withdrawal of the French Kampfgruppe built around I/ SS-Frw-Gren-Rgt 57. His officer-candidate status is indicated by officers' silver-cord edging to the collar patches displaying the SS runes and the rank insignia of senior sergeant – W-Oberscharführer. Note also the officer's silver crown piping on his M1943 field cap. (Chris Chatelet Collection)

Ceremonial opening of the LVF recruiting centre at Borgnis-Desbordes barracks, Versailles, on 27 August 1941. At right, in dark suit and holding his hat, is Pierre Laval, the *de-facto* premier of the Vichy government, who on this occasion was the subject of a failed assassination attempt by a member of a rival right-wing faction. (Chris Chatelet Collection)

was also distributed to be placed on the right side of the steel helmet, but only in minimal numbers (the Wehrmacht had already discontinued the German equivalent). On 5 October 1941, the French volunteers took an oath of allegiance to Hitler specifically 'in the fight against Bolshevism'. Once their rather hasty training was judged complete, at the end of October they left for the Eastern Front, arriving in Smolensk at the beginning of November.

THE EASTERN FRONT

In snowy weather on 6 November, a first column of the LVF left Smolensk for the front line facing Moscow, initially on foot with horse-drawn transport. After some 200km/125 miles, I Btl boarded trucks near Zarjewo, and for most of the way the columns followed the Minsk-Moscow highway.

Two bicycle couriers from the LVF's 5. Kompanie photographed in Smolensk in November 1941 – see Plate B2. (Chris Chatelet Collection)

Before even reaching the front line the Legion lost nearly 400 men to frostbite, dysentery and other illnesses, and morale and disipline were suffering from factional political quarrels. Once in the area of operations, the 638th Rgt was subordinated to 7. Infanterie-Division (GenLt Freiherr von Gablenz), in VII. Armee-Korps of AG Mitte (Army Group Centre). Under *Col* Labonne, with Hptm (Capt) Winneberger as German liaison officer, the regimental HQ staff was led by *Cdt* (Maj) Maurice Castan de Planard de Villeneuve, and the HQ Co (Stabskompanie) by Capt Tixier. I Bataillon, under Capt Louis Leclercq, included three rifle companies (1.-3. Kompanien) and a machine-gun company (4. Kp); II Btl (Capt André Girardeau) was similarly organized, with 5.-7. and 8. Kompanien. The regimental 13. (Infanterie-Geschütz – infantry-gun) Kp was led by Capt Michel Zègre, and 14. (Panzer-Jäger – anti-tank) Kp by Capt Albert Bouyol.

November–December 1941: Operation 'Typhoon'

From 22 November 1941, the 7. Inf-Div took part in the German offensive on Moscow. Despite crippling weather and a serious lack of supplies and adequate winter equipment, the Germans had already occupied the cities of Kaluga, Mozaysk and Rzev. Now, to allow two armoured concentrations (Guderian's Panzergruppe 2 advancing from the south, and Reinhardt's and Hoepner's Panzergruppen 3 and 4 from the north) to close their grip on Moscow, Gen von Kluge's 4. Armee was ordered to attack frontally to fix the greatest possible number of enemy forces. The 7. Inf-Div occupied a sector about 10km/ 6¼ miles wide in the Kubinka Lake region, some 70km/ 43½ miles SW of the Soviet capital.

On 24 November, with the LVF HQ established in Golowkowo, I Btl went into the line, its command having now passed to Maj de Planard due to Capt Leclercq's ill-health. On 1 December, while II Btl remained in reserve in the village of Arkangelsk, Gen von Gablenz ordered I Btl to capture and then defend the village of Djukowo on the lake of the same name. In temperatures of 40–60° below zero, Lt Jean Genest's 1. and Lt Jean Dupont's 2. Kpn would attack, supported by the MGs and mortars of Lt Charles Tenaille's 4. Kp, and with Lt Albert Douillet's 3. Kp in reserve. The 1. Kp advanced first through the snow-bound forest, and, despite suffering significant losses, managed to get close to Djukowo. The 2. Kp, following, were halted in a clearing by intense enemy fire; the attached MG platoon were mown down before they could get their guns into action, and only a few survivors managed to find cover in the forest. After waiting in vain for the arrival of 2. Kp, Lt Genest halted 1. Kp's attack and took up defensive positions. When Soviet units from the 32nd Siberian Inf Div attacked these the legionaries repelled the first assaults, but in the end only about 50 survivors of the two companies remained – a disastrous baptism of fire for the French volunteers.

With tanks, wheeled vehicles and heavy weapons disabled by deep snow and freezing temperatures, the German offensive halted just as Red Army reinforcements brought in from Siberia launched a counteroffensive along the entire front. During the defensive battles that followed, the German front broke down into a series of desperate fights by isolated units, weakened as much by frostbite and sickness as by combat casualties. On 5 December Soviet artillery pounded the LVF II Btl's positions in Arkangelsk, and on the 6th those of I Btl, killing Lts Tenaille and Dupont and seriously wounding the adjutant, Capt André Lacroix, among many others. That day, after holding some of their positions for a very long week, the survivors of I Btl had to be relieved, and regrouped with the regimental HQ in Golowkowo; it was only due to the skill and determination of a few officers and NCOs that a complete collapse was avoided. On 9 December another regiment of 7. Inf-Div came to relieve the exhausted II Bataillon. Three days later the LVF began to retreat towards Viazma as part of the German withdrawals on the Moscow front.

During December another contingent of 1,400 French volunteers (including some 200 black soldiers, partly of North African origin) arrived at Debica in Poland, where formation of a third battalion from new trainees was immediately started. The LVF in Russia now numbered only 565 all ranks, and II Btl had virtually ceased to exist.

Negative judgements

General von Gablenz wrote in his report: 'I do not think it will be possible to engage the French Legion after its relief... the training of the men needs to be improved, and therefore it must be transferred to the rear'. On 9 December, the opinion of Hptm von Tarbuk of VII. Armee-Korps staff was that 'The Legion numbers, for the most part, capable men of good spirit. The officers are in some cases too old, though some made a good impression. In its current state and structure, it is necessary that the LVF be led by German officers.'

On 23 December a more damning report was delivered by Obstlt (LtCol) Reichelt, head of operations for 7. Infanterie-Division. It read, in part: 'During the attack by 7th Inf Div on 1 December, intended to break up the enemy lakes sector, 1st French Legion Bn was to clear the woods south of the area after an artillery preparation.... The battalion reached its objective. Shortly after the start of the [subsequent] attack, there was a certain confusion between the elements. The heavy weapons were little or badly used. Some other forward progress was, however, successfully completed. On 3 December the 2nd Bn took over the positions of the [German] 19th Inf Rgt west of Lake Djukowo....

'Only on 6 December did the enemy begin intense patrolling activity; the men in the [French] outposts withdrew immediately, abandoning their weapons. [Controlling] the unit became impossible, and the battalion commander realized that he could no longer hold the position. As a result of the above events, the two battalions of the French Legion have been withdrawn from the front line.... The men are generally endowed with good will, but are not adequately prepared on a military level. The NCOs are good to some extent, but command at the top level is moronic. The officers are incompetent, [being] recruited according to political criteria.... The Legion is not fit to be engaged

Wartime postcard showing legionaries of the regiment's 13. (Infanterie-Geschütz) Kp in December 1941. The gun appears to be a 15cm sIG 33 of the company's single heavy platoon.

in combat. The reorganization must include the renewal of the officer corps, and an in-depth military education.'

On 24 January 1942, Army Group Centre's director of operations would submit to the Oberkommando des Heeres (OKH) a report judging that 'the state of the French Legion is such that it is considered necessary to reorganize it, before transferring it, or using it for security missions behind the front'. The Legion's significant losses in personnel and matériel were blamed partly on sickness but also on negligence, and the loss of heavy weapons on the unauthorized abandonment of positions. The men's morale was judged to be low; the troops had no confidence in their officers, and discipline left much to be desired.

January–February 1942: withdrawal, purge and re-formation

As early as 12 December 1941, the survivors of I Btl had left Golowkowo; despite his wound, Capt Lacroix assumed command of the unit, replacing the seriously ill Maj de Planard. On foot in the intense cold, since all vehicles and most horses had been lost, the legionaries had to march west for Viazma along the same route by which they had come. II Bataillon, under Capt Girardeau, followed more or less the same itinerary, but separately. From about 4 January 1942 both units paused in the vicinity of Kamenka, sheltering in civilian houses as best they could. From Kamenka, each company detached a number of men to hunt for partisans, who were very active. Colonel Labonne had installed his HQ in Wirutowo, where on 1 January 1942 he received 220 reinforcements.

On 7 January, I Btl resumed its march westwards; arriving in Zarjewo, NE of Viazma, it was at last loaded on to trucks and departed for Smolensk. On the 10th, II Btl received orders to follow it by the same route and methods. On 12 January, a provisional assignment order for the French regiment arrived from 403. Sicherungs-Division (GenLt Wolfgang von Ditfurth), one of two 'security' divisions under Army Group Centre. The LVF's HQ and I Btl were installed at Liesno, and II Btl at Saolscha.

December 1941: a legionary brings in a Red Army prisoner. Note that the LVF national sleeve patch was worn on the greatcoat as well as the tunic.

Once the LVF had been withdrawn from the front, many personnel were sent back to France for various reasons, including poor discipline and political quarrels as well as ill-health. A list was made of 16 officers to be repatriated immediately, including virtually all those over 40 years old – some on grounds of age, and others for their attitudes. At the same time, each of the two battalions was reduced from four to two companies; the 13. and 14. Kpn were dissolved for lack of equipment; and a purge of all LVF personnel took place, both in Russia and Poland.

All rankers over 30 years of age were excluded, such as older White Russian emigrés and German veterans of *la Légion Étrangère* (the French

Foreign Legion), and the African soldiers were also repatriated. At the same time, the German authorities sought to completely depoliticize those that remained, and the German liaison element was strengthened. Since they blamed the French for the loss of their horses, numerous Russian volunteer auxiliaries (Hilfswilligen) were attached to the LVF to handle the replacements, along with two German veterinaries per company. The companies received new motor vehicles (five trucks and three motorcycles each) to improve their mobility. From the total of 2,352 volunteers who had so far been sent up from Debica, the Legion now retained fewer than half: 1,096 all ranks, including 58 officers.

Towards the end of February the survivors of I and II Bataillone were transferred to Kruszyna, north of Radom in Poland, to be united in a re-formed I Bataillon. Although the new III Btl had already been formed, I and III Bataillone would remain autonomous units, and *Col* Labonne's regimental staff thus became superfluous. On 3 March 1942 five of the first eight Iron Crosses 2nd Class were presented, to *Col* Labonne (as a figleaf for his removal from command), and to four Frenchmen who had distinguished themselves in the December fighting: *Chef de bn* (Maj) Lacroix, *S/Lts* (2nd Lts) Maurice Pernel and Raymond Jeanvoine, and *Soldat* (Pte) Jean Villard. (The other three recipients were absent on convalescence.)

At the end of March 1942 about 750 French legionaries remained at Kruszyna, with whom the new I Btl, destined for anti-partisan operations ('Bandenkämpfung') behind the front lines, was formed under the command of Maj Lacroix. It had three rifle companies, and an HQ Co including a signals element, an anti-tank platoon (3x 3.7cm guns) and a mortar platoon (6x 8cm tubes). In early April two more groups of reinforcements from Debica arrived: a 'marching company' of 200 recovered wounded, and some 130 newly trained men.

May–June 1942: III Btl in the Volost valley

The LVF's new III Btl had already been engaged against the partisans for a month. Commanded by *Col* Albert Ducrot, this unit had been formed in December 1941 around a contingent of volunteers from France numbering 942 men. By February 1942 three more intakes had added

A cold and dirty LVF volunteer leads one of the unit's few remaining draught horses during the withdrawal of mid-December 1941, following the costly defeat near Lake Djukowo. (Chris Chatelet Collection)

another 480, but by April the German purge had reduced this total of 1,500-odd volunteers to only 624. The III Btl again had three rifle companies, commanded by Lt Lucien Mesléard (9. Kp), Lt Maurice Berret (10.), and Capt André Demessine (11.). The Stabs-Kp, commanded by Capt Michel Zègre, had a mortar platoon and an AT platoon, and the German liaison staff were led by an officer of field rank, Obstlt (LtCol) Wilhelm von Kirschbaum. When it left for the front, III Btl had 526 French and 44 German soldiers.

On 10 May the unit was posted to the Smolensk area to join 221. Sicherungs-Div (GenLt Johann Pflugbeil). At divisional HQ in Strigino on 16 May, *Col* Ducrot and ObstLt von Kirschbaum were warned for the unit's participation 'in an attack with the goal of eliminating the last Soviet elements which remain cut off from their lines since last winter. In the first line you will encounter partisans recruited locally, but organized militarily in regiments, battalions and companies. Behind them are regular troops from the 1st Guards Cavalry Corps, as well as paratroopers of the 4th Airborne Corps.' By nightfall on 20 May the companies, with the mortars and AT guns dispersed between them, had relieved the German reservists of Landesschützen-Btl 974 in outposts over a front of 4–5km/3 miles. Lieutenant Berret's 10. Kp was on the right in the village of Djatlowa, Capt Demessine's 11. on the left in Pawlowa, and Lt Mesléard's 9. Kp between them on a hill in front of Borodino. Battalion HQ was in Cholmy, with a platoon of three 'war booty' Renault light tanks, and a German 10.5cm artillery battery was in support at Rukino.

The battalion would remain in these positions for about 12 days. On the evening of 22 May, 10. Kp was attacked by enemy infantry supported by some light tanks, but these were driven off by the artillery. The days that followed were quiet except for occasional exchanges between artillery and snipers, while GenLt Pflugbeil planned a divisional offensive northwards towards the Jelnya-Smolensk railway line. This was to begin on 27 May, when 11. Kp was ordered to send out patrols to probe the enemy's strength and positions, but subsequently the start of the operation was postponed until 2 June. On 30 May, III Btl was attached to 221. Sicherungs-Div's Landesschützen-Rgt 45 (the future Sicherungs-Rgt 45), under the orders of Obst (Col) Johannes Wiesmann.

Their task was to sweep partisans out of the Volost river valley. On 3 June Obst Wiesmann ordered III Btl's 10. Kp (Lt Berret) to take Hill 249 north of Korjawki and Lt Mesléard's 9. Kp the hills near Galaschino, while Capt Demessine's 11. Kp waited in reserve in Pawlowa. The legionaries advanced at dawn, immediately clashing with partisan patrols. On an overlooking hill, *Col* Ducrot's command post came under enemy machine-gun fire. With German artillery support, both 10. and 9. Kpn achieved their objectives; the enemy were forced back, and a second ridge was reached. The division continued its advances on 4 June, when

Demessine's 11. Kp was ordered to push forward for about 3km/1¾ miles on the battalion's left, and then dig in to block Soviet forces dislocated by the advance of the Mesléard and Berret companies on his right.

Advancing at about 0200hrs in foggy darkness, Feldwebel *(Sgt-chef)* Jacques Seveau's lead platoon, followed by Demessine's command group with a mortar and an AT gun, came under fire while still in column formation. Too blind to manoeuvre, Seveau's platoon was pinned down in the open and took casualties. Somehow Capt Demessine managed to link up with Seveau, and to group his company in the open between the villages of Tschenzowo and Smorodina, where they repelled Soviet attacks from several directions. Feldwebel Seveau volunteered to make his way back to request support from the artillery and the other companies. While awaiting this, Demessine managed to get the bulk of his company on to a more defensible feature, but was soon so short of ammunition that his dozen MG34s each had only about one 200-round belt left. He had his men dig individual foxholes, and ordered them to husband their cartridges for certain hits at short range only. No reinforcements arrived, since both the other companies had been checked by enemy resistance, and repeated partisan attacks on 11. Kp reached hand-grenade range as the long day wore on. When darkness eventually fell, Capt Demessine managed to lead his men silently in single file back to Pawlowa, having suffered 16 men killed and about 40 wounded.

In his report, Obstlt von Kirschbaum complained that III Btl were 'courageous but unruly troops', who had advanced into territory infested with partisans without taking necessary precautions. However, his main criticism was of *Col* Ducrot, who 'completely lacks any aptitude for command and all the skills necessary for the wellbeing of troops'. Ducrot was dismissed; on the recommendation of Von Kirschbaum, his replacement was Capt Demessine, while Lt Georges Flamand took over 11. Kompanie.

On 8 June the offensive in the Volost valley was resumed. Still with Kampfgruppe Wiesmann, III/LVF initially combed the territory around the village of Pascino and subsequently over a wider area. They met no resistance, although the withdrawing partisans had left many mines and booby-traps behind them. On 14 June the 221.Sicherungs-Div, including *le bataillon Demessine*, received orders to transfer 230km/142 miles SW to the Gomel sector. Before they left, on 16 June Obst Wiemann decorated five French legionaries with the Iron Cross 2nd class: Chaplain Mayol de Lupé, Capt (soon to be Maj) Demessine, Medical Lt Moliniér, the promoted *Asp* (officer-candidate) Seveau, and *Soldat* Pellegrini. Between 6 July and 28 August, III Btl took part in the widespread anti-partisan Operations 'Vierek' and 'Eule', covering hundreds of square kilometres north of Gomel.

3 March 1942, Kruszyna camp, Poland, where the remnants of I and II/ LVF were merged into a new I Bataillon. These are two of the first eight Legion recipients of the Iron Cross 2nd Class for their conduct during the December fighting: (left) *S/Lt* Maurice Pernel, already wearing the ribbons of many French awards, and (right) *Soldat* Jean Villard. (Chris Chatelet Collection)

Volost valley, May–June 1942: sitting in the window, Lt Maurice Berret, commander of 10. Kp, III/ LVF. Berret would succeed to command of III Btl in February 1943 after the death of Maj Panné during Operation 'Marokko', and would survive to lead II/ W-Gren-Rgt 58 of the SS-Div 'Charlemagne' in February 1945. (Chris Chatelet Collection)

July–December 1942: I Btl returns to the front

After completing training, Maj Lacroix's re-formed I Btl was also sent to an operational area. The first convoy left Kruszyna on 17 July, carrying Lacroix with his 1. Kp (Capt Georges Cartaud), 2. (Lt Pierre Michel), and 3. (Lt Noël Piqué). A second convoy transported the German liaison staff under Hptm Winneberger, and the Stabs-Kp with a signals platoon, AT platoon (S/ Lt Jean Lemarquer) and mortar platoon (S/Lt Clément Samboeuf). Between 21 and 23 July the legionaries arrived – somewhat to their surprise – at Borisov, NW of Minsk in Belarus: Maj Lacroix had not made their rear-area anti-partisan mission widely known. The battalion was subordinated to 286. Sicherungs-Div (GenLt Johann-Georg Richert), tasked with security operations in the Smolensk area behind Army Group Centre (Gen von Schendorff) alongside 201., 203. and 221. Sicherungs-Divisionen.

The battalion started its first combing operation on 27–28 July, marching in column SE along the Beresina river to Nowoselki and Murowo led by the motorcyclists of the German liaison team; it then spread out from Murowo in repeated search operations over about the next ten days. On 1 August Gen von Schendorff flew to Borisov in person, and briefed Maj Lacroix that his battalion was to be responsible for the protection of river convoys passing on the Beresina. On 13 August, however, the unit was transferred to the area south of Vitebsk to take part in Operation 'Greif'. The 286. Sicherungs-Div, plus two German Police battalions and several of Russian volunteers, were sent against some 5,000 partisans believed to be holding the Vitebsk-Orscha-Smolensk triangle, where they were preying upon road and rail traffic. The French battalion advanced via Ostrow-Juyewo on 17 August, and the next day successfully captured the defended village of Osjerry. 'Greif' continued until early September, when I Btl returned to the Borisov region; the HQ settled in Smestii, with the rifle companies at Denisovici, Vidriza and Ucholoda.

Sub-units regularly had to carry out road-opening patrols to preserve the lines of communication and supply, and not always without cost. On 4 October a 20-man patrol led by SgtMaj Marchand, taking mail and supplies to points between 1. Kp at Denisovici and 2. Kp at Vidriza, fell into an ambush at the hamlet of Kalinin. They were massacred; when a column from the other direction reached the site, they found only 18 stripped and mutilated corpses. Therefter intensive search-and-destroy operations lasted into December. On 13 December 1942, Maj Lacroix (considered by the Germans to be too politically active) was repatriated to France, being replaced in the interim by Capt Henry Poisson.

September 1942–February 1943: III Btl at Krutojar and on the Desna

After a short period of rest, Maj Demessine's III/LVF went to relieve Sicherungs-Bataillon 743 in the protection of the much-sabotaged rail line between Unetscha and Kritschew, east of Krasnopolje.

The battalion staff and Stabs-Kp, German liaison staff and 9. Kp were installed in Kostjunowitschi, the 10. in Maryje-Bewelnkitschi, and the 11. in Bratkowitschi. In mid-September, 125 replacements arrived from Kruszyna.

On 25 November orders were given for the occupation of the strategic village of Krutojar, 6km/3¾ miles NE of Niwnoje, and on the morning of the 26th Stabsfw (Fr. *Adjudant*, Brit. Warrant Officer) Picard, leader of 9. Kp's 1st Ptn, set out. His group consisted of four combat squads, one of them from 10. Kp, with four MG34s and an 8cm mortar; a signaller and three other men from 9. Kp HQ, with a war correspondent, Cpl Bailly; and 25 Russian auxiliary policemen. Reaching Krutojar at about 0900hrs, Picard ordered his men to surround the village while the Russian police searched it. He then led them NE towards Degtjarewka, but at about 1130hrs they came under fire from dense woodland. His men were unable to make contact before the ambushers fled, and Picard then decided to return to Krutojar. About 500m short of that village, two parties totalling about 80 partisans were spotted; while Stabsfw Picard's men hastened to reach Krutojar the rearguard came under fire, and its seriously wounded Ogfr (Cpl) Pellegrini shot himself rather than be taken alive. Krutojar was attacked and mortared before the legionaries could organize a defence, so Picard led his men to Fedorowka, having suffered three killed, six wounded and six missing. The rest of 10. Kp, plus an element from Polizei-Rgt 8, then attempted to capture Krutojar, but were driven back to Niwnoje; this village was itself immediately attacked by the partisans, and was held only with difficulty. On 28 November Stabsfw Picard's combat group, the whole of 9. Kp and a company from I/ Polizei-Rgt 8 advanced to Krutojar once again, but found it undefended.

Volost valley, May–June 1942: surrounded by his men, Capt André Demessine (centre), who was awarded the Iron Cross for his leadership and extrication of his 11. Kp during an action on 4 June which cost it some 56 casualties. He was also promoted to major *(chef de bataillon)*, and given command of III/LVF in place of the dismissed *Col* Ducrot. (Chris Chatelet Collection)

This photo from a wartime book shows I/LVF crossing the Beresina river to take up positions in villages around Borisov on the east bank (an area with historic resonance for French soldiers since 1812). For several months from July 1942, the battalion was based there for anti-partisan duties under 286. Sicherungs-Division.

At the beginning of February 1943, III Btl, now commanded by Maj Eugène Panné, was transferred to the Desna river to take part in a German counteroffensive by 2. Panzer-Armee against a Soviet penetration between Orel and Kursk. The battalion HQ and 11. Kp were installed in Ostraya Louka; to the left, 9. Kp occupied the village of Gvinelo in contact with a Hungarian unit, while 10. Kp in Dolsk were in touch with an Ostbataillon of Kirghiz volunteers. Red Army units were solidly dug in on the far bank of the Desna, but gave no sign of offensive intentions, although French and Soviet reconaissance patrols clashed. Subsequently the armoured speahead of 2. Panzer-Armee enclosed this Soviet force in a pocket which was then annihilated by infantry, including the French battalion.

Ambushes, June–August 1943

From the beginning of June 1943 the two battalions of the LVF, both under 286.Sicherungs-Div, were operating in the same sector: between Borisov and Tolocin to the north, the Tolocin–Krugloje–Moghilev road to the east, and the course of the Beresina river up to Murovo to the west. I Bataillon was stationed in the western region of this sector, and III Btl in the east. Major Panné's III Btl HQ was in Krugloje, with its companies, linked by regular patrols, in other villages facing constantly moving bands of partisans. Captain Raymond Dewitte's 10. Kp was particularly heavily engaged.

On 9 June divisional HQ requested that 10. Kp provide protection for engineers repairing telephone lines cut by partisans on the Moghilev-Bobruisk road beyond the Vaprinka river. A single truckload of 16 men was sent along the forest road without any advance reconnaissance – positively inviting ambush – and only the Russian auxiliary truck-driver escaped the inevitable carnage. When relief patrols arrived they found 16 naked corpses around the looted and burnt-out truck, some showing evidence of terrible deaths. This incident heralded the start of increased partisan activity in the French battalion's sector along the course of the Beresina. It prompted the formation of a special 'hunting' element (*groupe de chasse*, led by the now S/ Lt Jacques Seveau) independent of the rifle companies, to specialize in prompt intervention and aggressive hit-and-run strikes against partisan-held villages.

On 5 July 1943 the Germans launched their massive Operation 'Zitadelle' against the Soviet Kursk salient. The Red Army was well informed in advance; among their preparations, large partisan forces were mobilized to harass the German lines of communication, and the LVF III Btl's dispersed companies consequently saw hard fighting. On 18 July partisans attacked the village of Kolbovo continuously for 12 hours before being driven off. On 1 August it was the turn of Dubovoje, which was also held, though at a cost of some 20 casualties. On the night of 7/8 August, 11. Kp at first defended a position near Orechovka, then counterattacked successfully.

On 11 August the newly-arrived Capt Ernest Estel was escorting a supply-wagon column between Sokolovici and Novopolje with some 100 men: about half of 9. Kp from Dubovoje, and other legionaries returning from leave. About halfway along their route signs of mining were spotted, and the column halted to check. A sceptical legionary jumped on one of the disturbed patches in the dirt road, and was immediately blown to pieces, whereupon ambushers opened fire with machine guns and mortars. The inexperienced Capt Estel was one of the first to be killed; the wooden wagons offered no useful cover, and although men tried to shelter in houses beside the track, and Lt Bérard led a desperate bayonet charge, all the legionaries were either killed outright or after the partisans reached the wounded. This ambush was the most costly action for III Btl during the whole of 1943.

On 27 August 1943, the second anniversary of the formation of the LVF, the Legion received a new flag. Resembling the French 1879 regulation regimental pattern, it now bore the battle-honours '1941–1942 DJUKOWO' and '1942–1943 BERESINA'.

For repeated acts of courage and resourcefulness, Jacques Seveau of III Btl was promoted through the ranks from Feldwebel to Oberleutnant, being awarded the Iron Cross 1st Class for successfully leading the unit's *groupe de chasse* at Solovitchy in December 1943. In this photo from a wartime book, note the buttonhole ribbons of the Iron Cross 2nd Class and Winter 1941/42 medal, and the French tricolour shield hand-painted on Lt Seveau's helmet for lack of an issue decal.

THE LEGION REBORN

September–November 1943: back to regimental status

In autumn 1943 the formation of a new II Btl (Maj Jean Tramu) brought the LVF up to regimental strength once again. This unit was officially established in November 1943, from newly trained volunteers. The three battalions were then unified into a regiment under the command of Col Edgar Puaud, a seasoned *Chasseurs Alpins* and *Infanterie de Ligne* veteran of World War I and, with the *Légion Étrangère,* of interwar colonial campaigns (and recently chief-of-staff of the *Légion Tricolore* in France – see below, and Plate D1). The regiment's order-of-battle in September–November was as follows:

Kommandeur: Col Edgar Puaud
Stabs-Kompanie: Capt Henri Guiraud
I Bataillon:
   Btl-Kdr: Capt Jean Bassomperre
   1. Kp: Capt Jean Boudet-Gheusi
   2. Kp: Lt Alfred Falcy
   3. Kp: Lt Noël Piqué
II Btl:
   Btl-Kdr: Maj Jean Tramu
   5. Kp: Lt Guillaume Vewybraes
   6. Kp: Capt Jean-Marie Pruvost
   7. Kp: Lt Roger Audibert
III Btl:
   Btl-Kdr: Maj Eugène Panné
   9. Kp: Lt Raymond Gaillard; Nov 1943 > Lt Bernard Boillot
   10. Kp: Lt Bernard Boillot; Nov 1943 > Lt Maurice Berret
   11. Kp: Lt Jean Neveux

October 1943–February 1944: Solovitchy, the Somry forest, and Operation 'Marokko'

Meanwhile, at the beginning of October and November 1943 respectively, III Btl (Maj Panné) and I Btl (now, Capt Bridoux) participated in operations to eliminate partisan bands east of the Beresina. At the start of December, French patrols identified Solovitchy as an important hub of partisan communications and logistics. A combat group including two platoons of 10. Kp and S/Lt Seveau's *groupe de chasse* from III/LVF was formed to ambush an anticipated partisan column there.

In a temperature of 20° below, the legionaries approached the village by night and took positions along the road that passed through it. A group of enemy carts soon approached, and were wiped out with MG and mortar fire. However, Seveau judged that this was only an advance party for the larger column that had been reported, and cleared the road of wreckage and corpses in order to resct his ambush. A more numerous column indeed arrived at Solovitchy some hours later; waiting until it was completely within the ambush zone, Seveau gave the signal to open fire, and once again his mortars wrecked the wagons while MG crossfire raked the partisans. They tried to mount a counterattack, but in the end all were shot down. Running short of ammunition and with wounded to carry, Seveau then withdrew, sparing the enemy wounded. For this action he was promoted to first lieutenant and decorated with the Iron Cross 1st Class.

From 27 January 1944 all three LVF battalions took part in the same operation for the first time. The German command believed that up to 6,000 partisans were sheltering in the Somry forest, where an airstrip SW of Saoserje allowed their resupply with weapons

Photo from a wartime book showing French volunteers in action in overgrown terrain. Their usual escort and patrol missions in 1942–43 meant that they often had to fight encounter actions in thick country against stronger forces of Soviet partisans, who – resupplied by the Red Army, and sometimes reinforced by regular Red Army paratroops – were routinely equipped with machine guns and mortars.

and ammunition, and where they had been reinforced by Red Army regular paratroops over the past weeks. Several German Army battalions were committed, together with Russian volunteer Ostbataillonen. On 30 January elements of III/LVF attacked the defended village of Kosel frontally without waiting for preparatory mortar fire, supported from the left by the rest of the battalion and from the right by part of I Bataillon. This shock attack took them up to the first houses, where return fire forced them to take cover in the snow; at that point they received support from the mortars and from German 15cm artillery in the rear. The village began to burn, forcing its defenders into the open under French MG fire, and a counterattack from the last intact houses was stopped dead. The combing-out of the Somry Forest and its surroundings continued for about 15 days.

Taking advantage of a temporary eastwards retreat by the bulk of the partisans, the German command authorized a new encirclement attempt, planned with *Col* Puaud and named, in compliment to a previous chapter in his career, Operation 'Marokko'. On 15 February 1944 the LVF units were driven along the Bobruisk–Moghilev road. Pivoting on the village of Cecerici, the French then wheeled 90° to the SE, getting behind the enemy forces, and the following day moved westwards to take them between two fires. They inflicted much damage and many casualties; the cost was light, although on 18 February III Btl's Maj Panné fell in combat, to be replaced by Capt Berret. Although the bulk of the enemy once again managed to withdraw, the OKW bulletin was positive, reporting about 1,200 partisans killed and 1,400 captured.

I Bataillon then headed north to return to its sector east of the Beresina. While on the march on 26 February it fell into a major ambush while passing through thick cover near Devoscizi, but this time the legionaries' quick reactions were successful. Captain Bridoux immediately spread his men along the margins of the forest, and got the mortars and AT guns into action fast. After three hours' fighting the ambushers withdrew, despite their superior numbers, and Capt Bridoux would be rewarded with promotion to *chef de bataillon*. In mid-May 1944, *Col* Puaud returned from a month-long recruitment drive in France, bringing with him a company's-worth of volunteers. With the addition of local recruits, these would form a 13th rifle company (Capt Émile Aiffray) as the embryo of a planned but never formed IV Bataillon.

June 1944: the Marty column

On 11 June a column was sent from Novo Polessy towards Krutchka, through woodland where partisan activity was reported. Under the orders of Capt Marty, it comprised some 130 men: two platoons from I Btl's 3. Kp (Lt Yves Rigeade), and a cavalry platoon (Sgt Gabin).

Accompanying the column was I Btl's CO, Maj Bridoux, who was returning to his HQ at Sokolovici. To cover the movement of the column, Col Puaud sent about 60 men from the regimental Stabs-Kompanie, under Capt Henri Guiraud, to meet up with Marty north of Krutchka. After a quiet start, Marty's scouts noted suspicious movements ahead, and he moved his column off the road to continue through the fringes of the surrounding woodland. While fording a stream shortly before their rendezvous point with Capt Guiraud, they came under heavy fire. The French managed to place their machine guns and respond, but many legionaries fell. Given the enemy's superior strength, and the revealed presence not only of partisans but also of Red Army paratroopers, Maj Bridoux ordered a leapfrogging withdrawal through the brush, covered by successive rearguards. At one point a French counterattack led by Lt Rigearde drove back the leading pursuers. Taking advantage of this respite, Bridoux and some of his men managed to reach Novo Polessy, where he radioed the alarm to regimental HQ, and also to divisional HQ in Krupka calling for immediate armoured support. This was not sent, but at 1300hrs a German company with a couple of MG-armed trucks arrived, and the enemy were driven back. It was discovered that Capt Guiraud's force had been ambushed at 0800hrs and completely annihilated. In total, the French had lost more than 100 dead or missing in the woods around Krutchka.

Operation 'Bagration': the defence of Bobr

On 22 June, a massive Red Army offensive struck Army Group Centre. This Operation 'Bagration' also involved intensified partisan activity behind the German front, and thousands of explosions cut the railway lines and major bridges all the way from the Dniepr river back to the area west of Minsk. While the German front lines were smashed open, their rear areas collapsed in confusion and retreat. Having crossed the Bobr river, Col Puaud's LVF was then ordered to recross it and cover the retreat of other units. A 600-strong Kampfgruppe was formed for this purpose under the orders of Maj Bridoux and the head of the German liaison staff, Oberst von Spee; this comprised the whole I Btl, two companies from III Btl, the new 13. Kp, and the AT element.

Arriving at the village of Bobr, some of the French took up positions in front of the road bridge over the river, where some defences had already been built along the Minsk–Moscow highway. Lieutenant Rigeade placed

Captain Jean Bridoux, commander of I/LVF November 1943–July 1944, photographed wearing French M1939 uniform. Although almost certainly a political appointee (his father was the Vichy minister of war), he rose to the rank of major for competent leadership in combats culminating in the desperate defence of Bobr, near Minsk, in June 1944. However, his rank reverted to captain (Waffen-Hauptsturmführer) when the LVF was absorbed into the Waffen-SS as part of the 'Charlemagne' Bde in August 1944. (From wartime magazine *'Journal de Normandie'*, August 1943)

his 3. Kp with the heavy MGs in the village cemetery. The 2. Kp, with the heavy mortar platoon, settled in trenches linking up to the highway, and the AT guns were emplaced on the right of the road to the village – good defensive positions, on elevated ground overlooking the approaches. Oberst von Spee managed to persuade the commander of a platoon of Tiger tanks to reinforce the Kampfgruppe; two Tigers were camouflaged in the forest edge, while the other two were placed beside the highway. On 24 June, Soviet tanks arrived before the French positions, but halted to await their infantry before attacking. The powerful, long-ranged 88cm cannon of the four Tigers destroyed the Soviet tanks one by one, while the French mortars and MGs put the infantry to flight. During the night, strong elements of an SS-Police regiment, including some 7.5cm AT guns, also arrived.

At dawn on 26 June, Soviet artillery began to pound the defenders' positions, and was soon enhanced by Katyusha rocket-launchers. Immediately following this barrage Soviet infantry attacked the village, first hitting 3. Kp in the cemetery. The attack was repulsed, but Lt Rigeade took a serious head wound, and was replaced by S/Lt Michel de Genuillac. After a period of relative quiet the Soviets returned to the attack, this time with about 50 T-34s and Shermans. The Tigers opened fire at long range, and numbers of Soviet tanks were later also knocked out by the 7.5cm guns. Their hulks soon blocked some of the routes of advance for the rest; only six tanks managed to get close, of which four were destroyed by the Tigers and the other two at short range by the LVF's 3.7cm 'doorknockers'.

At 2300hrs on the 26th a renewed assault in force captured Bobr cemetery, annihilating its defenders. The Tigers again stopped the enemy tanks, giving the French a chance to counterattack, and the cemetery was recaptured in furious hand-to-hand fighting. At dawn on the 27th the Soviets assaulted yet again, in even greater numbers of armour and infantry. The Tigers and the French infantry's heavy weapons continued to take their toll. Three Soviet tanks managed to reach the cemetery, but the 3.7cm guns hidden

A late LVF recruiting poster from early 1944, boasting of its exploits 'For France and Europe' during three winters in Russia.

there under the orders of Lt Piqué destroyed two; Piqué himself fell in the act of engaging the third. By 0800hrs the Soviets had established themselves north of the cemetery and along the railway line, and at 0900 they were clearly preparing for another assault when Col Puaud arrived with orders to withdraw.

Despite the violence of the fighting, the LVF recorded relatively modest losses: 41 killed and 24 wounded. No fewer than 57 Soviet tanks had been knocked out, and the plain in front of the village was scattered with hundreds of dead infantrymen. The LVF's three-day delay of the Soviet advance had allowed the orderly retreat of other German units, and the evacuation of thousands of wounded from hospitals in Borisov and Minsk. On 28 June, a ridiculous but flattering Red Army press release claimed that 'On the Bobr river, armoured units belonging to the 2nd Byelorussian Front were stopped by the fierce resistance of two French divisions'.

July 1944: Minsk

Hitler had ordered a stubborn defence of the Beresina river, and the LVF was among the units committed to holding a bridgehead on the east bank in front of Borisov. On the afternoon of 28 June, Lt Jean Fatin was in place along the highway east of Borisov with his 1.Kp and survivors of III Btl, and that night Maj Bridoux recovered the other two companies of I Btl south of Laonitza. Meanwhile II Btl (Maj Tramu) had escaped encirclement at Moghilev to head towards Belynici, where they covered the retreat of the Panzergrenadier-Division 'Feldhernhalle'. In the Borisov bridgehead Lt Fatin's command, short of equipment and ammunition, fought off the enemy until 30 June, when Col Puaud arived to lead their withdrawal westwards in person. The legionaries of II Btl from Belynici crossed the Beresina to join the other remnants, which regrouped a few kilometres east of Minsk. On 1 July the Red Army began to tighten its grip around the city from the NE and SE, and Puaud received the order to commit his men to Minsk's defence, but on 3 July the Soviets penetrated Minsk, and the French – now down to about half strength – retreated westwards.

Starting on 9 July, all the LVF survivors were withdrawn from the front and shipped to Kaunas in Lithuania, where they remained until the 15th. From 18 July they were sent to the Greiffenberg training area in East Prussia. It was there that the Germans began the process of gathering all categories of their French volunteers – willing or not – into the Waffen-SS (see below).

LA LÉGION TRICOLORE

In the summer of 1942, Pierre Laval was seeking ways to strengthen the French forces available to defend French national interests in all theatres. Considering the LVF to have become 'too German', the Vichy government decided to form its own national legion. On 22 June 1942 it offically announced the absorption of the LVF within a newly created *Légion Tricolore*. A major propaganda and recruitment campaign was launched, aimed particularly at veterans of 1940, the LVF, *l'Armée de l'Armistice* and *l'Armée d'Afrique*. Command of the LT was given to a 'commissioner general', Gen Paul Galy, with an experienced Foreign Legion officer, LtCol Edgar Puaud, as chief-of-staff. (For operational purposes the Germans simply ignored the French claim to control the LVF, since Verstaerktes Französische Inf-Rgt 638 was a Wehrmacht unit.)

Volunteers from the Occupied Zone were gathered at the LVF's La Reine barracks in Versailles, and those from the Unoccupied Zone at Des Augustines barracks in Guéret. At these depots they were issued French M1938 khaki uniform, later distinguished by an embroidered right-breast shield bearing the Napoleonic eagle (although, despite Darnand's boast on 12 July, German *feldgrau* was in fact envisaged for use in war zones). On 28 August 1942 Otto Abetz, the German ambassador to France, attended a ceremony in Paris formalizing the birth of the Tricolour Legion. However, the German military

Lieutenant-Colonel Edgar Puaud was a former NCO who was commissioned via the St Maixent academy into the *Chasseurs Alpins* in 1914, and was decorated during World War I. He left the Army in 1919, but in 1923 Capt Puaud was accepted into the *Légion Étrangère,* and served in Morocco, the Levant and Indochina. In July 1942 he joined the *Légion Tricolore,* becoming its chief-of-staff; here he wears an M1939 French officer's tunic with LT staff insignia, and a mourning band – though not, on this occasion, the LT breast badge seen in other photos. Compare with Plate D1. (Chris Chatelet Collection)

Reportedly taken on 25 August 1942 at the Quartier des Augustines barracks at Guéret, this shows enlisted men of the *Légion Tricolore.* Depending upon the exact subject, place and date, photos show much variation in insignia – see also Plate E1. (Chris Chatelet Collection)

showed no interest in either enlarging or easing the operational limits on the Armistice Army; shortly after this ceremony the Wehrmacht high command reiterated its decision to recognize only the LVF as a French voluntary military formation, and refused to supply the Tricolour Legion with weapons or helmets for training. Assembly and training of volunteers nevertheless continued.

On 10 November 1942, only three days after the Allied Operation 'Torch' landings in French Morocco and Algeria, the local Vichy commander Adm Darlan signed an armistice. Consequently, the Germans and Italians quickly occupied the whole of the previously Unoccupied Zone, and disbanded Vichy's Armistice Army and with it the *Légion Tricolore.* During 1943 some of the latter's personnel, including LtCol Puaud, went to join the ranks of the LVF in Russia, while part of the LT infrastructure in France was retained to service the LVF.

LA PHALANGE AFRICAINE

A minor consequence of the 'Torch' landings, and of *l'Armée d'Afrique's* rapidly switching its allegiance to the Allied side in the war, was the creation of *la Phalange Africaine* ('the African Phalanx'). Despite the local armistice many Frenchmen in North Africa remained loyal to Vichy, and took encouragement from the fact that as early as 9 November German and Italian reinforcements began landings in Tunisia which would continue by air and sea. The Axis military proceeded to occupy the whole of northern Tunisia, to which GenFM Rommel was retreating westwards from Libya with his mauled Panzerarmee Afrika after its defeat by the British at El Alamein. The German authorities asked Vichy to make a greater military commitment, and on 21 November Joseph Darnand made a radio appeal in France for volunteers for the reconquest of North Africa from the Allies. Recruiting offices were opened, and by the end of November some 700 volunteers had applied

A first-pattern embroidered breast shield of the *Légion Tricolore*; see also Plate H4. The eagle might be gold flecked with brown, as here, or white flecked with gold. (Chris Chatelet Collection)

Late December 1942: Adml Ésteva, the French resident-general in Tunisia, greets two officers of the military mission sent out to organize local recruiting for the *Phalange Africaine*. Here, both Maj Curnier (left) and Capt Peltier display the *Phalange's* double-bladed axe badge on the right breast – see Plate H5. Just visible in the background is SS-Stubaf (Maj) Zeitschel of the SIPO and SD. (Chris Chatelet Collection)

to join, including ex-members of the newly disbanded Armistice Army and Tricolour Legion.

Since the Mediterranean was now relatively unsafe for Axis maritime convoys, the Germans also decided to allow the direct recruitment of volunteers in Tunisia. A French military mission, led by LtCol Pierre Cristofini and Maj Henri Curnier, flew in on 28 December 1942. Their main aim was to recruit from among French veterans and members of units which at that time had been more-or-less abandoned to their own devices, and a local recruitment office was opened on 1 January 1943.

Kompanie Frankonia

Only a matter of days later a first (if largely symbolic) unit was announced. This so-called 'Kompanie Frankonia' was quartered at Forgemol barracks in Tunis city, and on 2 February 1943 it was sent to Bordj-Ceda camp on the coast for training. Among the white settler volunteers were nationalist militants, students and demobilized career soldiers. At first the strength was reportedly about two-thirds white and one-third Tunisian and Algerian Arabs and Berbers, but the Germans ordered the exclusion of the latter. During February the company was rebuilt almost entirely from members of the SOL veterans' organization, and would be commanded by its local deputy chief, Capt André Dupuis.

At the end of February the company was officially formed, with six officers, 42 NCOs and 212 rankers. Designated by the Wehrmacht as the Franzosische Freiwilligen Legion, it was attached to II Btl (Hptm Michael Bürgmeister) of Grenadier-Rgt 754 of the newly-arrived 334. Infanterie-Division. Weapons were a mixture of French and German rifles, with 18 French light machine guns; the heavy platoon had four French Hotchkiss MGs, two 60mm mortars, and three 47mm AT guns. German instructors, mainly veterans of the Eastern Front, were attached to supervise the training, in collaboration with a German paratroop company commanded by Lt von Bülow. At an official ceremony on 18 March the volunteers swore on the French flag their allegiance both to Pétain as French head of state, and to Hitler as supreme commander of the German Wehrmacht. By that date they numbered some 250 men, of whom about 176 would go into the line while the rest remained in the rear on service and training duties.

From 2 April 1943, the *Phalange Africaine* company was officially assigned to 334. Inf-Div (GenLt Friedrich Weber). On the night of 8/9 April, six platoons were driven to join the division in the front line near the village of Medjez El-Bab. Facing them were elements of the 78th Inf Div of British First Army. The company were subjected to shelling and aerial bombing, losing their first killed and wounded on 14 April. On the night of 16/17 April volunteers led by SgtMaj Picot, supported by a German squad, reported a successful clash about 4–5km/3 miles to the east with a patrol supposedly of either New Zealand

(continued on page 33)

LÉGION DES VOLONTAIRES FRANÇAISES, 1941–42
1: *Col* Labonne; France, 7 Sept 1941
2: *Soldat;* Debica, Poland, Oct 1941
3: *Sergent* replacement; Poland, early 1942

A

LÉGION DES VOLONTAIRES FRANÇAISES, 1941–42
1: *Sergent-chef*; Smolensk, Nov 1941
2: Cyclist courier, 5. Kp; Smolensk, Nov 1941
3: *Soldat,* Moscow front, Dec 1941

B

LVF PERSONALITIES
1: *Col* Edgar Puaud, 1943-44
2: *Monsignor* de Mayol de Lupé, 1943
3: *Lieutenant* Jaques Doriot, 1944

LÉGION TRICOLORE, 1942–43
1: *Artilleur,* Paris, 27 Aug 1942
2: *Aspirant, École des cadres;* Guéret, spring 1943
3: *Sous-lieutenant;* Russia, summer 1943

E

**PHALANGES AFRICAINE
& NORD-AFRICAINE, 1943–44**
1: *Volontaire*, PA; Tunis, Jan 1943
2: *Capt* Dupuis, PA; Vichy, May 1943
3: *Volontaire*, PNA; Dordogne, 1944

FRENCH WAFFEN-SS
1: W-Oscha Henri Fenet; SS-Junkerschule Bad Tölz, Dec 1943
2: W-Osch, I/ W-Gren-Rgt 57; Galicia, Aug 1944
3: W-Rof, Sturmbataillon 'Charlemagne'; Berlin, Apr 1945

INSIGNIA & DECORATION
See commentary text

1

2

3

4

5

6

7

8

Charlemagne

H

or Indian troops. Picot was killed, as were seven Allied soldiers, and the French and Germans took three wounded prisoners. For propaganda purposes this episode earned them the remarkable reward of no fewer than three Iron Crosses and a mention in 334. Inf-Div's war diary.

On the night of 22/23 April, British batteries shelled the adjoining positions of III/Gren-Rgt 754, and from 0400hrs switched targets to the French company. A few hours later British tanks and infantry assaulted; a whole German company was wiped out, leaving a breach in the defensive front through which attackers surrounded the French positions on Hill 119. The French would report about 60 casualties (though nearly all listed as 'missing'), and on 27 April they were withdrawn into reserve. They retreated ever further eastwards, suffering several aerial attacks, and numbered only about 60 men when, on 6 May, they regrouped in Tunis. On German orders, Capt Dupuis disbanded his company and told them to try to escape individually. Only a few French officers managed to board Axis aircraft for Italy, and most of their men surrendered at Cap Bon on 8 May. Their losses in action were reported as six killed, seven wounded, but 57 missing. Many of the prisoners were released, others were sentenced to terms of imprisonment by French courts, and 14 of them (12 French and two Arabs and/or Berbers) were convicted of treason and shot.

FRENCH VOLUNTEERS IN THE WAFFEN-SS

Creation of the French brigade

Since 1940, in the aftermath of the Franco–German armistice, individual French volunteers had been welcomed into the Waffen-SS, especially men from Alsace and Lorraine of German family origin, and including others who travelled to Brussels or Antwerp in order to enlist more discreetly. From December 1942, by which time their numbers had reached a few hundred, Himmler suggested to Hitler the formation of a complete SS unit of French volunteers. This plan was mentioned in an internal SS circular on 3 March 1943. The creation of a French Waffen-SS unit was endorsed by the Vichy government on 22 June, confirmed by Hitler on 18 September, and immediately recorded by the SS High Command (SS-FHA). Two days after this official announcement, almost 1,500 applicants showed up at the Waffen-SS's Paris recruiting office in Avenue du Recteur Poincaré.

By 30 September some 800 had been accepted to begin training at Cernay (Sennheim) in Alsace, while future specialists were sent to various Waffen-SS training schools. From 10 January 1944, 28 former French Army officers attended a shortened course at the Bad Tölz SS-Junkerschule, directed by SS-Hstuf (Capt) Erich Kostenbader. At the end of January 1944, 2,480 Frenchmen were recorded in the Waffen-SS. In March, the volunteers were transferred to Neweklau camp, near Prague, where they were organized into a two-battalion infantry regiment. On 22 January this was initially designated SS-Frw-Gren-Rgt 57 (französische nr.1) – which apparently was also sometimes prematurely referred to as the Französische Brigade der SS. It was commanded by W-Stubaf (Maj) Paul Gamory-Dubourdeau, assisted by SS-Hstuf (Capt) Kostenbader and the German liaison officer, SS-Ostuf (Lt) Hans-Ulrich Reiche.

October 1943: Some of the first 800 French volunteers for the Waffen-SS to arrive at Sennheim (Cernay) training camp in Alsace. Behind the German instructors, most are still in civilian clothing, but several wear the dark blue uniform of the *Milice Française*, which provided significant numbers of volunteers. (Chris Chatelet Collection)

(The German SS guarded its exclusive prestige jealously. Rather than using the simple 'SS-' prefix of German units and personnel, later-war foreign formations and ranks within them were prefixed with 'Waffen-', meaning 'Armed' – e.g., 'W-Stubaf' = Waffen-Sturmbannführer, 'foreign SS major' – and formation titles were suffixed 'der SS'.)

On 30 June 1944 the formation numbered 1,688 (30 officers, 44 NCOs and 1,614 rankers), but only five companies were ready for employment at the front. The other rifle (now 'grenadier') companies, the 'pioneer' (combat engineer), signals, AA and AT sub-units, and many specialist NCOs, were all still undergoing training. Nevertheless, during June the formation had been designated 8. SS-Freiwilligen-Sturmbrigade (8th SS Volunteer Assault Bde), during a brief period when several such brigades were temporarily given ordinal numbers. It seems to have reverted to Französische SS-Frw-Sturmbrigade by the end of July, when it received orders to create a battle group for combat deployment to the East. The brigade's II Btl would remain in Neweklau under the orders of W-Stubaf Gamory-Dubordeau, while the battle group was based on I Btl, to which a light infantry element, a pioneer squadron and an AT platoon were added. The order-of-battle of the Kampfgruppe, roughly 1,000 strong, was as follows:

Btl-Kdr: W-Hstuf (Capt) Pierre Cance
Ord-Offz: W-Ustuf (2nd Lt) Dominique Scapula
IVb: W-Ostuf (Lt) Dr Pierre Bonnefoy

Stabs-Kp: W-Ostuf Jean Croisile
1. Kp: W-Ostuf Noël de Tissot
2. Kp: W Ustuf Léon Gaultier
3. Kp: W-Ostuf Henri Fenet
le Inf-Kol: W-Ustuf Maugny
Pi-Schwdr: W-Oscha (SgtMaj) Gomez
PzJäg-Zug: W-OJ (Officer Candidate) Henri Kreis.

August 1944: the Galician front

'*Le Bataillon Cance*' left Neweklau on 30 July 1944 for the Sanok sector of the Galician front, where it joined SS-Kampfgruppe 'Schäfer', which was itself built around SS-PzGren-Rgt 40 of the 18. SS-Frw-PzGren-Div 'Horst Wessel'. On 9 August the French 3. Kp was the first to be committed, filling a breach between other positions. Sent up the next day, the other companies were heavily shelled while marching through the Dundukami woods; among the casualties was 2. Kp's seriously wounded W-Ustuf Gaultier, who was replaced by W-Ostuf Joseph Pleyber. After consolidating its positions, on 12 August the battalion launched a successful counterattack towards the Cracovia-Sanok railway line. On 19 August the French SS unit was transferred along the Visloka river to the Mielec sector, 100km/62 miles NW of Sanok.

The following day a heavy Soviet offensive penetrated the front for about 10km, and, under threat of encirclement, Cance's battalion fell back that evening. Waffen-Oberjunker Kreis's AT platoon managed to hold the village of Radomysl until 1900hrs, but the retreat in the face of greatly superior numbers cost the battalion dearly; by the evening of 22 August it had only about 300 men still able to fight, mostly in separated platoons. Waffen-Obersturmführer De Tissot was killed, and elements of the 1. and 3. Kpn were grouped by W-OJ Abel Chapy to link up with other units of Kampfgruppe 'Schäfer' in front of Dubrowka. In the village of Mokre (where a war correspondent, W-Ostuf Jean Le Marquet, distinguished himself in combat) the battalion staff and most of 2. Kp under W-Ustuf Lambert fought desperately to repel Red Army attacks; W-Hstuf Cance was seriously wounded, to be replaced by W-Ostuf Croisile, and Reiche, Lambert and Le Marquet all fell. In fact, all the unit's officers had been either killed or wounded by the time about 140 survivors finally regrouped in the Tarnow forest. Those killed numbered 137 (including seven officers), the wounded 669, and 40 men were missing. Members of the French battalion group would subsequently receive 58 Iron Crosses, many of them posthumous.

On 24 August, W-Ostuf Croisile reorganized the survivors in three nominal companies, under W-Stabs-OJ Chapy, W-Ustuf Bartolomei, and W-Oscha Lefèvre. These were ordered to make their way to the Schwarnegast region in eastern Pomerania, where II Btl of the Sturmbrigade was then located.

THE 'CHARLEMAGNE' DIVISION
August–October 1944: reorganization
While I Btl of the Sturmbrigade served in Galicia, II Btl had been transferred to Schwarnegast and Bruss, NE of Konitz in Pomerania. Not far away, at Greiffenberg in East Prussia, were the veterans of the LVF.

The French Waffen-SS sleeve shield, as issued (initially to the German cadre) at Neweklau training camp in March–July 1944. (Many veterans of the LVF retained the Army shield.) This is a very rare RZM-marked example. (René Chavez Collection)

Galician front, summer 1944: (left to right) SS-Ustuf Reiche, the German liaison officer of the French battalion group; SS-Stubaf Schäfer, commanding its parent Kampfgruppe from 18. SS-Frw-PzGren-Div 'Horst Wessel'; and W-Hstuf Pierre Cance, commanding the reinforced I Btl from the French SS-Frw-Sturmbrigade. (US NARA)

On 10 August the LVF was officially transferred from the Army into the Waffen-SS and, together with the former Sturmbrigade, it would now constitute the Waffen-Grenadier-Brigade der SS 'Charlemagne' (französische nr.1), taking its honour-title from the great 9th-century Frankish emperor. Two regiments were formed: from the Sturmbrigade, W-Gren-Rgt der SS 57 (W-Ostubaf (LtCol) Gamory-Dubordeaux), and, from the LVF veterans plus some French tranfers, W-Gren-Rgt der SS 58 (W-Hstuf Bridoux). Command of the 'Charlemagne' Bde was initially given to W-Oberf (BrigGen) Puaud, but, while remaining on the staff, from 10 October he was superseded by an officer with longer seniority in general officer's rank, the fluent French-speaker SS-Brigaf (MajGen) Dr Gustav Krukenberg. Training of the reorganized French units was led by SS-Staf (Col) Walter Zimmermann. During October the two infantry regiments completed their training at Schwarnegast and Saalesch, and an AA battery (W-Ustuf René Fayard) was attached.

On 26 October 1944 the 'Charlemagne' Bde was transferred to Wildflecken training ground, where it was reinforced from Ulm with some 1,800 members of the *Milice Française,* fleeing Free French vengeance in their liberated country. Subsequently, the brigade was transformed (on paper) into a division, becoming the W-Gren-Div der SS 'Charlemagne' (französische nr. 1). No published source gives an official date for this change, but the vacant divisional number '33.' was assigned only on 10 February 1945. The effectives of the new division reached about 7,300 men, with approximate numbers from the following sources: Organization Todt and NSKK, 2,300; *Milice Française,* 1,800; LVF, 1,200; SS-Frw-Sturmbrigade, 1,100; and Kriegsmarine, 640. An 'Honour Company' was also formed under a German officer, SS-Ostuf Wilhelm Weber.

Many members of the division were sent to attend specialist training schools, and general training continued throughout January 1945, although hampered by shortages of weapons, equipment and even rations. In mid-February it was decided to transfer the division to the Hammerstein training ground in Pomerania, where it was supposed to receive its heavy weapons. In the meantime, command of W-Gren-Rgts 57 and 58 had passed to W-Hstuf Victor de Bourmont and W-Stubaf Emile Raybaud respectively.

February–March 1945: the Pomeranian front

On 17 February the division's units left Wildflecken and were transferred NE by train. The military situation between the Vistula and the Oder river lines had become critical, with battles raging in East Prussia and Pomerania. On 15 February, 3. Panzerarmee elements had struck down from Pomerania into the right flank of Gen Zhukov's vast offensive towards the lower Oder, convincing him that his 1st and Gen Rokossovsky's 2nd Byelorussian Fronts must swing north into Pomerania before they resumed their final drive on Berlin.

On 22 February, the first elements of W-Gren-Rgt der SS 57 arrived at Hammerstein station, and were placed at the disposal of XVIII Gebirgs-Korps (Gen Hochbaum), committed to defending the Hammerstein-Landeck sector. The I/ 57 (W-Ostuf Fenet) took up position in Heinrichwalde, II/ 57 (W-Hstuf Obitz) in Barkenfelde, and W-Hstuf de Bourmont's regimental HQ in Bärenwalde. Almost as soon as they arrived, the French SS grenadiers were attacked by the leading elements of massive Soviet forces driving NW towards the Baltic coast, whose assaults would break the French formation into three scattered parts and nearly destroy them.

Waffen-Grenadier-Regiment 57 was forced to fall back on the Bärenwalde-Hammerstein railway line, and the arrival of I/ 58 (W-Hstuf Emile Monneuse) from Wildflecken was insufficient to prevent the front from collapsing. The II/ 58 (W-Hstuf Berret) was the next to face attack; on the afternoon of 26 February their AT guns managed to knock out some Soviet tanks, but the Red Army continued to punch through the defences in great strength. About 3,000 men led by W-Oberf Puaud took up positions around Barenhütte, but were soon driven out. Another group from W-Gren-Rgt 57 fell back northwards towards the castle of Elsenau, where SS-Brigaf Krukenberg's HQ was located, and other isolated elements continued to fight independently. In front of Elsenau, SS-Ostuf Weber's Honour Company destroyed 18 Soviet tanks, while W-Hstuf Robert Roy's gunners knocked out at least 14 more, but in all the day's fighting cost the division a reported 500 killed and 1,000 missing, plus numerous wounded.

Galician front, August 1944: a French crew from the Cance Battalion's HQ Company serving an 8cm mortar in action. (US NARA)

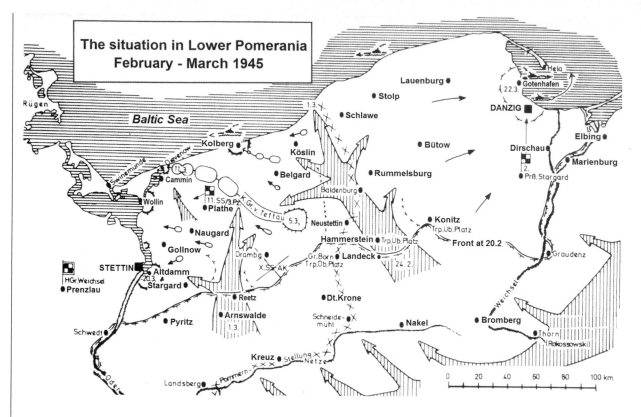

The situation in Lower Pomerania
February - March 1945

On the evening of 26 February the 'Charlemagne' survivors began to fall back to Neustettin, where they received the modest reinforcement of 150 men under the orders of W-Ostuf Bassompierre, and part of SS-Flak-Batterie 33 under W-Ustuf Fayard.

On 29 February the units in Neustettin were reorganized. Some formed a 'march battalion' under the ordnance officer, W-Ostuf Auphan, who was ordered simply to delay the Soviet advance for as long as possible. The next day, in intense cold, the bulk of the division's survivors withdrew northwards for about 80km/50 miles, then being joined by SS-Replacement Bn (Ersatz-Btl) 33 under SS-Staf Zimmermann. On 2 March, the division was reorganized yet again: a two-battalion 'march regiment' of the best remaining men would be led by W-Stubaf Raybaud, with W-Ostuf Fenet and W-Ostuf Bassompierre as battalion commanders, while the tiredest and most demoralized became a 'reserve regiment' (W-Hstuf de Bourmont). On the night of 3/4 March, in complete confusion, all took defensive positions around Köslin, subordinated to an *ad hoc* Korps 'Munzel', but Köslin fell on the 4th.

On 4 March the Soviets reached Kolberg on the Baltic Sea coast; hard fighting resumed, during which W-Stubaf Raybaud was seriously wounded, and the French units then tried to fall back south-east towards Belgard. Leading the column with SS-Brigaf Krukenberg's staff was I Marsch-Btl (W-Ostuf Fenet), followed by the two 'reserve' battalions (W-Hstuf Monneuse and W-Ostuf Devefer) and W-Oberf Puaud, with II Marsch-Btl (W-Ostuf Bassompierre) as rearguard. Early on 5 March, using the cover of darkness, I Marsch-Btl arrived in front of Belgard, and then turned north-westwards. However, a large gap had by now opened up between them and De Bourmont's 'reserve'.

In daylight but thick fog, W-Oberf Puaud decided to keep marching along the Persante river, but during the morning the fog cleared, exposing the column to the Red Army on a bare plain. What followed was a massacre, led by Soviet tanks and artillery; the French fell in their hundreds, most of the survivors simply fled into the forest, and both W-Oberf Puaud and W-Hstuf de Bourmont disappeared amid the chaos. Trying to escape along the Köslin-Belgard railway, II Marsch-Btl was engaged in a series of furious fights before W-Ostuf Bassompierre and many of his men were captured a few days later. As for the divisional staff and W-Ostuf Fenet's I Marsch-Btl, after a punishing five-day march they managed to reach the Baltic coast at Horst. On the beach they were joined by thousands of civilian refugees, who accompanied them westwards along the coast until they reached German lines at Dievenow on 12 March. The next day 500-odd French survivors were shipped west to Swinemünde at the mouth of the Oder delta.

March–April 1945: final reorganizations

From 15 March, I Marsch-Btl, the divisional staff, and some straggling groups led by W-Stubaf Jean Boudet-Gheusi were assembled in the Altdamm sector. The division's survivors were now structured as a single W-Gren-Rgt der SS 'Charlemagne', nominally under the command of SS-Staf Zimmermann (in fact he had been wounded in Pomerania, and would be lost when his evacuation ship was sunk). On 21 March they left for Neustrelitz, in the Mecklenburg Lakes region. On 24 March SS-Brigaf Krukenberg installed his HQ in Carpin, where the regiment was divided into two battalions: SS-Btl 57 (W-Hstuf Fenet), including the veterans of the Sturmbrigade, was located in Bergfeld, and SS-Btl 58 (W-Ostuf Jean-Baptiste Géromini) near Grunow, while the survivors of the Honour Co were quartered in Ollendorf. Over the following week stragglers, wounded discharged from hospitals, and specialists returning from their courses all rejoined the regiment at Carpin. This increase in effectives obliged SS-Btl 57 to move to Fürstensee, and SS-Btl 58 to Wokuhl. However, at the beginning of April serious internal tensions – between those still willing to fight on, and those who were utterly demoralized – forced yet another reorganization.

Volunteers who were determined to continue fighting included most of the 'Weber' (Honour) Co, three-quarters of SS-Btl 57 and about half of SS-Btl 58; these diehards were grouped in one 'heavy' and two 'assault' battalions, and received new clothing, equipment and weapons. The rest – about 400 men, including many former *Miliciens* – were formed into an unarmed labour unit (Baubataillon), under W-Hstuf Roy. This left its quarters on 27 April, and eventually dispersed in small groups to try to reach and surrender to the Western Allies.

The remnant 'Charlemagne' Rgt, commanded by SS-Hstuf Kroepsch, had a 'heavy battalion' (W-Stubaf Boudet-Gheusi), which was equipped with Panzerschreck and Panzerfaust hand-held AT weapons, and also included pioneer and signals platoons, a medical element and a re-fuelling column. The rebuilt SS-Btl 57 (W-Hstuf Fenet) comprised three grenadier companies (W-Ustuf Jean Labourdette, W-Ostuf Pierre Michel and W-Oscha Jean Olliver). Now commanded by SS-Hstuf Hans-Robert Jauss, a German officer from 11. SS 'Nordland' Div, SS-Btl 58 also had three companies (W-Ostuf Fatin, W-Hscha Rostaing and W-Ustuf Leune), while Weber's Honour Co was renamed SS-Kampfschule ('battle

Emile Raybaud, photographed for a wartime magazine in the uniform of a *Milice Française* departmental or regional *chef*. With the rank of W-Sturmbannführer, he commanded the 'Charlemagne' Div's W-Gren-Rgt 58 in Pomerania in February 1945, and from 2 March a 'march regiment' assembled from various remnants. On 4 March he was severely wounded during the loss of Kolberg.

Waffen-SS 'grenadier' (the German title for 'infantryman' from November 1942) armed with a single-shot Panzerfaust short-range anti-tank rocket launcher. These were available in large numbers by 1945, and would be used to great effect by the Sturmbataillon 'Charlemagne' in Berlin. (US NARA)

school') 33. During April about 20 French officer-cadets from the Kienschlag academy were integrated into SS-Btl 58. Throughout the regiment the French volunteers were issued good numbers of Panzerfausts, new Sturmgewehr 44 assault rifles and MG42s.

April–May 1945: Berlin

On the night of 23/24 April, the SS-FHA ordered SS-Brigaf Krukenberg to Berlin to take command of the remnant of 11. Frw-PzGren-Div 'Nordland', badly mauled on the Oder front.The German capital was now on the point of being encircled by Gen Zhukov's 1st Byelorussian Front from the north and Gen Konev's 1st Ukrainian Front from the south, and was already under heavy-artillery fire. Krukenberg decided to take his French volunteers with him, but could only find enough transport for some of them. The meagre truck convoy he scraped together carried Fenet's SS-Btl 57, Rostaing's 6. Kp from SS-Btl 58, and Weber's Kampfschule.

This column followed a roundabout route southwards, but still suffered from air attack. At 2200hrs on 24 April, shortly before the Soviet ring closed around the city, just under 330 men arrived near the Olympic stadium. On 25 April, SS-Brigaf Krukenberg took command of the Danish and Norwegian 'Nordland' remnants, to which he attached the French unit, and received his orders. He was officially subordinated to LVI. Panzer-Korps (Gen Weidling), but the actual chain-of-command on the ground was confused and disputable, and in practice Krukenberg would look for orders to SS-Brigaf Wilhelm Möhnke, commanding the central area around the Reichs Chancellery and its Führerbunker. The 'Nordland' was deployed in Defence Area C, the SE defences, and was at first positioned just south of the Landwehr Canal, NE of Tempelhof airfield. On 25 April the French volunteers were incorporated into a single Sturmbataillon: a reduced HQ (W-IIstuf Fenet), four companies each about 65 strong, plus the Kampfschule. After reaching the Hermannplatz, they entered combat at around 1200hrs on the 26th. Making a counterattack SE down Braunauerstrasse, supported by a handful of 'Nordland' Div assault guns and by a few King Tiger tanks, the grenadiers destroyed at least 14 Soviet tanks at close range, but W-Ostuf Michel was among those killed. Despite the Red Army's vast superiority of numbers, close-quarter street-fighting among badly damaged buildings is always a costly 'meat-grinder' of men and equipment, and Red Army losses would be consistently high.

On 26/27 April, under northwards pressure from Gen Chuikov's 8th Guards Army, Krukenberg's men were pulled back over the canal into Defence Area Z in the heart of Berlin. They now held a line from

Spittelmarkt to Belle-Alliance Platz, with Krukenberg's command post at first in the cellars of the State Opera on Unter den Linden, later in the Air Ministry on Wilhelmstrasse, and finally in the Stadtmitte U-bahn (underground railway) station close to the ruined Potsdamer Bahnhof. At some point W-Hstuf Fenet was wounded, but continued to lead the battalion, and Möhnke awarded him the Knight's Cross on 29 April (one of three men of the battalion to be so honoured).

Now separate from the 'Nordland' survivors, the French volunteers continued their desperate resistance, knocking out more Soviet tanks but being steadily worn down in numbers; among the fallen was W-Ustuf Labourdette, killed while covering a tactical withdrawal by his company. They made the Red Army pay for every building and street-corner, but on the 28th the attackers reached to within a few hundred metres of the Reichs Chancellery. The French soldiers resisted until 1/2 May, but on the 2nd most of those who were still alive (sources vary, between 60 and 120 men) were finally captured near the Potsdamer station, on their seventh day of non-stop fighting.

The other remnants of the division

After the massacre on the Belgard plain on 5 March about 600 men, mostly from the division's service and logistical elements, managed to reach the port of Kolberg. There SS-Ostuf Paul Ludwig, formerly a German liaison officer with the LVF, and a Swiss officer, SS-Ustuf Heinrich Büeler, managed to assemble a solid 200-strong march company. This was attached to the makeshift Paratroop Bn 'Hempel' for the defence of the 'pocket' against Soviet and Polish attacks until 18 March, when about 30 survivors managed to take ship for Swinemünde. From there they were sent to Wildflecken, where they would be integrated into the *ad-hoc* SS-Rgt 'Hersche' (see below) at the end of the month.

The retreat in Pomerania, February 1945. These troops appear to wear the thin white snow-camouflage parka and trousers issued in 1943/44 to be worn over the grey Waffen-SS padded winter combat clothing. (US NARA)

Dr Gustav Krukenberg photographed as a German Army field officer; although a pre-war member of the Allgemeine-SS, ObstLt Krukenberg did not transfer to the Waffen-SS until December 1943. After the destruction of his command in Berlin on 2 May 1945 he managed to evade capture for a week, but would then spend 11 years in Soviet imprisonment. (US NARA)

Other elements of 'Charlemagne', isolated during the February fighting at Elsenau and Bärenwalde, followed a German retreat to the north-east. From 3 March, in Schlawe, W-Hstuf Obitz, commanding II/W-Gren-Rgt 57, grouped survivors of his unit with part of W-Ostuf Fatin's isolated 1./W-Gren-Rgt 58, and 100 artillerymen of W-Art Abt der SS 33 led by W-Hstuf Martin. During a train journey to Neustadt about 50 were killed in a Soviet air-raid on Stolp station, including W-Ustuf Philippe Colnion, commander of 8./W-Gren-Rgt 57. Obitz himself was wounded; evacuated by sea, he too lost his life when his ship was sunk. Arriving at Neustadt, NE of Lauenburg, on 6 March, W-Hstuf Martin then organized three companies to retreat towards Danzig. On 20 March, Martin's command was (confusingly) renamed SS-Ersatz-Bataillon 33; subordinated to 4. SS-Polizei-PzGren-Div, it suffered heavy losses NE of Gotenhafen. On 1 April, some 100 survivors were shipped to the Hela peninsula, and thence to Copenhagen on 5 April. About another 100, led by W-Ostuf Fatin, were directed to Neustrelitz, where they joined SS-Brigaf Krukenberg's W-Gren-Rgt der SS 'Charlemagne'.

The latter, after the departure of its Sturmbataillon for Berlin, still had about 700 soldiers at Carpin under the orders of W-Stubaf Boudet-Gheusi. The bulk were from SS-Bn 58 (SS-Hstuf Kroepsch), in three companies commanded by W-Ostuf Fatin, W-Ustuf Maxime Leune and W-StdJ Pierre Aumon. On 27 April, with Soviet armour about 15km/9 miles away, Boudet-Gheusi transferred his HQ to Zinow. After delaying the advance of the Soviets at Carpin and Fürstensee, on 30 April the French volunteers retreated westwards, and on 1 May they arrived in the Wismar sector. The following day most of them surrendered to British troops.

Finally, about 1,200 French recruits were under training at Wildflecken, which was evacuated in the face of advancing US forces. On the night of 30/31 March, the French SS volunteers were organized as a 'march regiment' under SS-Ostubaf Heinrich Hersche. This included a nominally motorized battalion (SS-Stubaf Katzian) of three companies, and a 'special' battalion (SS-Stubaf Erich von Lölhöffel) consisting of two labour companies and a penal company. On 1 April, when about 60km/37 miles from Wildfleken, the SS-Rgt 'Hersche' was forced by the approach of American tanks to continue retreating, via Eispheld, Sonneberg and Kronach, reaching Hof on 13 April. From there, the senior general SS-Ogruf Gottlob Berger ordered the French regiment to march on to join the defence of the planned last-ditch 'Alpine Redoubt'. On 14 April the regiment, 600 strong, reached Regensburg. Some elements saw combat near Wartenberg, others in front of Moosburg, subordinated to the 3,000-strong 38. SS-Gren-Div 'Nibelungen' formed from shreds of other destroyed formations. Most retreated south via Rosenheim, and were captured at Lofer, Austria; others preferred to aim for Italy by way of the Brenner Pass, but surrendered to the Allies in the South Tyrol.

BIBLIOGRAPHY

PRIMARY SOURCES:
Public archives
Bundesmilitär-archiv (Freiburg, Germany)
Berlin Document Center (Berlin, Germany)
US National Archives and Records Administration (NARA, Washington, DC)

Wartime publications
Magazine *Das Schwarze Korps*
Magazine *Signal*
Magazine *Stuttgart Jllustriertei*
Magazine *Devenir*, 1944

Books
LVF: legion des volontaires français contre le bolchevisme (1943)
La Waffen-SS, Armée de la nouvelle Europe (1943)
La SS t'appelle (1943)

POST-WAR WORKS:
French volunteers
Afiero, M., *I volontari stranieri di Hitler* (Ritter Editrice; Milan, 2001)
Afiero, M., *La Crociata contro il bolscevismo. Vol 1: le legioni volontarie europee* (Marvia Editrice)
Afiero, M., *Divisione Charlemagne* (Marvia Editrice)
Afiero, M., *11.SS-Frw.Gren Div. 'Nordland'* (Associazione Culturale Ritterkreuz)
Aron, R., *The Vichy Regime 1940-44* (Boston; G.P. Putnam, 1958)
Destampes, B. & Tellechea, H., 'La LVF en Biélorussie juin-juillet 1943' in *Militaria* No.222 (Histoire et Collections; Paris, Jan 2004)
Forbes, R., *For Europe: the French Volunteers of the Waffen-SS* (Helion & Co Ltd)

Lambert, P. P. & Le Marec, G., *Les français sous le casque allemand* (Jacques Grancher Editeur)
Landwehr, R., *French Volunteers of the Waffen-SS* (Siegrunen Edition)
Lefèvre, E., 'La Croix de Guerre LVF' in *Militaria* No.12 (H et C; Aug/Sept 1986)
Lefèvre, E., 'La LVF et la Légion Tricolore' in *Militaria* No.21 (H et C; June 1987)
Leguérendais, C., *Sotto le insegne del Terzo Reich* (L'Assalto Edizioni)
Mabire, J. & Lefèvre, E., *La légion perdue, face aux partisans 1942* (Éditions Grancher)
Mabire, J., *Brigade Frankreich* (Ed. Fayard; Paris, 1973)
Mabire, J., *La Division Charlemagne* (Ed. Fayard; Paris, 1974)
Mabire, J., *Mourir a Berlin* (Ed. Fayard; Paris, 1975)

Waffen-SS
P. Antill, *Berlin 1945*, Campaign 159 (Osprey Publishing; Oxford, 2005)
K.W. Estes, *A European Anabasis: Western European Volunteers in the German Army and SS, 1940-1945* (Columbia University Press)
P. Hausser, *Waffen SS im Einsatz* Oldendorf, 1953)
E. G. Kraetschmer, *Die Ritterkreuztraeger der Waffen-SS* (Preussisch Oldendorf, 1982)
D. Littlejohn, *Foreign Legions of the Third Reich, Vol 1* (R. James Bender Publishing; San Jose, 1979)
R. Lumsden, *La vera storia delle SS* (Newton & Compton Editori)
H.W.Neulen, *An deutscher Seite, Internationale Froiwillige von Wehrmacht und Waffen SS* (Universitas, 1985)
G.H. Stein, *The Waffen-SS: Hitler's Elite Guard at War 1939-1945* (Cornell University Press)
G. Tessin, *Verbande und truppen der deutschen Wermacht und Waffen-SS* (Biblio Verlag)
H. Werner, *Verbande und truppen der deutschen Wermacht und Waffen-SS* (Biblio Verlag)
G. Williamson, *Storia Illustrata delle SS* (Newton & Compton Editori)

Red Army troops fighting in the streets of central Berlin, late April 1945. The fallen sign for 'Möltkestrasse' identifies the location as the Königsplatz in front of the Reichstag building, which was itself captured on the night of 30 April/1 May; the feature at the right may be the edge of an anti-tank ditch dug across the Königsplatz. In the left foreground, the long-barrelled 76.2mm ZiS 3 divisional field gun emphacizes the Red Army's deployment of artillery in street-fighting. (US NARA)

PLATE COMMENTARIES

A: LÉGION DES VOLONTAIRES FRANÇAISES, 1941-42

A1: *Colonel* Roger Labonne, France, September 1941

For the flag presentation parade, Labonne wears the service uniform of an Oberst in the Deutsches Heer, with the helmet worn when parading with troops. His M1935 tunic has collar-facing in dark green 'badge cloth', and the eagle-and-swastika *Hoheitsabzeichen* on his right breast is emboidered in silver on dark green. The silver *Litzen* collar-patch bars have infantry-white 'lights', and his interwoven silver-cord field officers' shoulder straps, with two 4-point gold rank stars, have white underlay. The German-made French national sleeve shield of 'heraldic' shape was only issued from October 1941, and Labonne displays a rare early French-made version; larger, and of simple shape rounded at the bottom, it bears the superscription 'FRANCE' in yellow on a white strip.

A2: *Soldat*; Debica, Poland, October 1941

This volunteer during training has been issued a German Army infantry private's M1940 uniform, with a field-grey collar; equally, the dark green M1938 shoulder straps were meant to be replaced with field-grey versions, but were often retained. His German-issue national sleeve patch is machine-woven on a field-grey background. This type was by far the most common, but small numbers of minor variations are known, including with dark green backing, and, very rarely, in printed form. This soldier 'presents arms' in the French manner, as was common practice.

A3: *Sergent* replacement, early 1942

During the rebuilding of the LVF after its partial destruction in December 1941, a batch of replacements travelled from France to Debica for uniforming, equipping and training, and thence to join the regiment at Kruszyna in April 1942. This figure represents their appearance on leaving France, wearing the khaki French M1935 *bonnet de police* and M1938 uniform. The tunic displayed no collar patches, but NCOs sported non-regulation brass grenade collar badges, as here.

B: LÉGION DES VOLONTAIRES FRANÇAISES, WINTER 1941/42

B1: *Sergent-chef* with regimental flag; Smolensk, Russia, November 1941

On their arrival at Smolensk the LVF were photographed parading their regimental flag. This Feldwebel, holding it for his subaltern officer before the three-man flag party go on parade, wears the standard-issue field-grey greatcoat with shoulder straps of rank, but no French sleeve-patch. However, his M1940 helmet displays one of the rarely issued decals of the French tricolour shield. The flag is a gold-fringed tricolour, lettered in gold 'LÉGION/ DES/ VOLONTAIRES' (obverse) and 'HONNEUR/ ET/ PATRIE' (reverse). A short tricolour cravat with gold-fringed ends is tied in a bow below the spearhead finial.

B2: Cyclist courier, 5. Kompanie; Smolensk, November 1941

The only protective winter items issued are a woollen tube-shaped 'balaclava' and three-finger mittens. He wears puttees and ankle boots instead of standard-issue German marching boots. Note that he has modified his German greatcoat by adding buttons and buttonholes to enable him to fasten the skirt-tails back in the traditional French Army manner for marching order. He carries his 7.92mm *Karabiner 98k* rifle slung.

B3: *Soldat*, Moscow front, December 1941

In the worst of the 1941/42 winter weather, all Wehrmacht troops wore whatever protection they could lay hands on or improvise. Apart from the 'balaclava' and mittens, the only winter items issued to them were thicker underwear, a round- or V-necked woollen sweater, and, as unit stores, a long, full-cut and warmly lined sentry's watchcoat, and straw overboots. In practice men wore layers of whatever they could find including all kinds of civilian items, fleece or fur garments being particularly prized. This Frenchman has acquired a civilian cap and large gauntlet mittens attached by a cord.

C: BYELORUSSIA, SUMMER 1943

In June–July 1943 a propaganda tour was made by the leading Vichy diplomat Fernand de Brinon (who was also president of the Central Committee of the LVF) to I/ and III/ LVF during their anti-partisan operations in the regions between Minsk and Smolensk. His entourage included Propaganda-Kompanie cameramen who filmed the French volunteers 'in action', and the footage was widely shown in newsreels (e.g. *Deutsche Wochenschau* of 7 July 1943).

C1: *Lieutenant*

Equivalent to an Oberleutnant, this company commander wears the M1938 officers' field cap, with silver piping around the top ridges and the frontal cut-out of the flap, and an infantry-white chevron of 'Russia braid' around the frontal

Colonel Roger Labonne, the first commander of the LVF, wearing the uniform of an Oberst in the German Army for this portrait in a wartime book. His national sleeve shield is an early privately-made variant (see Plate A1). In 1918 Labonne had commanded a battalion of the much-decorated Morocco Colonial Infantry Regiment (RICM), but by 1941 he was a 60-year-old retired officer with a history professorship but no relevant operational experience. This photo dates from March 1942, when Labonne was recalled to France and the LVF's regimental staff was discontinued until late 1943.

cockade. Unusually, he displays the gilt metal regimental number '638' on his shoulder straps, although this was forbidden in the field. Although the officers' regulation weapon was a semi-automatic pistol, junior leaders might often acquire a 9mm MP40 sub-machine gun. This subaltern is evidently a veteran of French colonial service; in addition to his French leather buckled leggings, he retains a traditional *chèche* white desert scarf.

C2: *Caporal-chef*

The marshy country flanking some parts of the Beresina river, where the LVF operated, was humid in the spring and summer, and infested with insects. This squad leader has an issue *Moskitonetze* in fine green mesh covering his helmeted head; this could be tightened around the bottom with a drawstring. He wears the shoulder straps of Unteroffizier's rank, and he too is armed with an MP40, carrying on his belt six spare magazines in two triple-pocket canvas pouches.

C3: *Soldat* with grenade-launcher

Although it took practice to master firing it with any accuracy, especially in thick woodland, the 30mm rifle-grenade attachment for the Mauser rifle (*K98k Gewehrgranatengerät*) was a useful addition to the rifle platoon's firepower. It consisted of a two-part tubular muzzle attachment, and a ramp sight clamped behind the rifle's rearsight on the left (though experienced soldiers usually judged the firing angle by eye). This *'Schiessbecher'* took anti-personnel, anti-tank and illumination rounds, propelled by firing a special rifle cartridge. The muzzle attachment, rear sight and spanner were carried in a black leather belt-pouch.

D: LVF PERSONALITIES

D1: *Colonel* Edgar Puaud, 1943-44

Originally a sergeant who was commissioned at the beginning of World War I, Puaud was a decorated veteran of the Western Front and, with the *Légion Étrangère*, of interwar colonial service. In July 1942 he joined the *Légion Tricolore*, becoming its chief-of-staff, and after its dissolution he was given command of the enlarged *Légion des Volontaires Français* in Russia in September 1943, instilling it with renewed determination. As a Waffen-SS brigadier-general and, in practice, deputy commander of the 'Charlemagne' Div, Puaud was badly wounded at Belgard in Pomerania in March 1945; he was subsequently abandoned in a village near Köslin with other casualties, and his fate is unknown. Here he wears the service dress of an Oberst of infantry, with both his French and German decorations; note the cross of a *Commandeur de la Légion d'Honneur* hanging at his throat.

D2: *Monsignor* Jean, Comte de Mayol de Lupé, 1943

Although he was 68 when he enlisted in the LVF in 1942, this Roman Catholic chaplain was present at all the Legion's battles on the Eastern Front, often accompanying companies in the field, and was awarded both classes of the Iron Cross. He was later one of the main architects of the transfer of French volunteers from the German Army into the Waffen-SS. After his capture in 1945 he was sentenced to 15 years' imprisonment, but was released on health grounds in 1951. He is illustrated wearing a chaplain's greatcoat, but with the lapels closed so that it resembles the standard officers' pattern; for formal duty the lapels were worn open to reveal violet interior facings, in the same way that general officers displayed red facings. Chaplains wore no shoulder straps on any uniform garment, but displayed the usual officers' tunic collar patches, with the silver *Litzen* on violet backing rather

Volunteers of 11. Kp, III/ LVF photographed in about June 1942. Under magnification, it can be seen that the central soldier has the letters 'LVF' embroidered across his sleeve shield – probably an individual choice or *'fantaisie'*. (Chris Chatelet Collection)

than dark green. The other distinctions of a chaplain (*Heerespfarrer*), either Catholic or Protestant, were: violet *Waffenfarbe*, and a silver 'Gothic' cross below the eagle badge, on the *Schirmmütze*; and a pin-on brass pectoral crucifix worn with a silver neck-chain. The officers' field belt was worn, but no weapons were carried.

D3: *Lieutenant* Jaques Doriot, 1944

Doriot was remarkable for being a senior pre-war figure in the French Communist Party before changing sides to support the Nazis, after being expelled by the Party over a doctrinal dispute in 1934. In 1936 he formed the quasi-fascist *Parti Populaire Français* (PPF), and in 1940 the mobilized SgtMaj Doriot won a second *Croix de Guerre* to add to the first awarded in 1917. A founder-member of the LVF, he received his former rank before leaving Debica for the front; by spring 1942 Lt Doriot was intelligence officer of III/ LVF, and in 1943 he received the Iron Cross 2nd Class. Allowed to remain active with the PPF and to attend conferences in France, he was killed by a strafing Allied aircraft in Germany in February 1945. His uniform here is the service dress of an infantry Oberleutnant, with the LVF armshield (obscured here) and his personal decorations.

E: LÉGION TRICOLORE, 1942–43

E1: *Artilleur*; Paris, 27 August 1942

This volunteer is a member of the first contingent of the LT to be transferred from Guéret in the Unoccupied Zone to Versailles. He wears a khaki beret without a badge, and M1938 uniform with *Légion Tricolore* insignia. It was initially planned that the LT should form a tactical brigade and, while this was never achieved, the collar patches anticipated it. For artillery, as here, they were scarlet, and for all branches they bore in khaki a horizontal diamond-shape above a *demi-brigade* number '1' or

'2'. All ranks wore the distinctive right-breast badge, this first pattern being embroidered – see photo on page 24, and Plate H4.

E2: *Aspirant, École des cadres de la LVF*; Guéret, spring 1943

The Vichy government's original order of 22 June 1942 announcing the absorption of the LVF into the *Légion Tricolore*, and that of 28 December 1942, dissolving the LT and reviving the official identity of the LVF, caused much confusion. One unit which was retained after the dissolution, and continued to display LT insignia, was this school for training future LVF platoon leaders. This officer-candidate (note rank insignia above his cuffs) wears M1938 uniform, with a khaki beret (often seen with an unauthorized horizontal gilt grenade badge). The collar patches are *bleu clair* with triple gold *soutaches* and a numeral '1', '2' or '3'. The LT's breast badge is still worn, but now with a plain machine-woven gold-yellow eagle thinly outlined in gold (or red and gold) within the edge of a black backing shield. Weapons were in very short supply; this student examines a German MP28/II sub-machine gun.

E3: *Sous-lieutenant*; Russia, June-July 1943

This is based on 2nd Lt Servant, photographed in the entourage of Fernand Brinon and LtCol Puaud during their visit to the LVF (see Plate C). He wears the black and *garance*-red infantry officers' M1935 *képi* with the single gold *soutache* of this rank but without a frontal badge. On his M1938 tunic, the diamond-shaped *bleu ciel* collar patches with gold *soutaches* and *grenade* identify him as a member of the former LT brigade staff. His single short 'campaign' gold rank bars are worn above the cuffs, and the LT embroidered badge on his right breast pocket. Servant was then the director of the LVF veterans' association, and displays the *Croix de Guerre Légionnaire avec palme* (see Plate H7), and the buttonhole ribbon of the German Eastern Front Winter

Monsignor **Jean, Comte de Mayol de Lupé (see Plate D2) was a member of the Vatican curia and a close friend of the Pope, who enlisted in the LVF aged 68 in order to provide spiritual care for the Frenchmen who volunteered to fight against the atheist Bolsheviks. (Chris Chatelet Collection)**

1941/42 Medal. Note that he wears a German Army enlisted ranks' belt and buckle, presumably a souvenir of 1941.

F: PHALANGES AFRICAINE & NORD-AFRICAINE, 1943–44

F1: *Volontaire*, PA; Tunis, January 1943

Although it was reported that some 150 local Arabs and/or Berbers enlisted during the initial recruitment drive for the PA, their service was brief. This volunteer has received the French khaki woollen M1938 *tenue de drap*, identified only by the PA's double-bladed *francisque* axe badge on the right breast (see Plate H5); a khaki-painted German helmet; and an M1917 belt and pouches. Later the French volunteers would apparently be issued sand-khaki *tenue de toile*, German khaki greatcoats, and German tropical boots. Reportedly, at least some of the helmets were carefully hand-painted with a tricolour shield on the right side and the *francisque* shield in black and white on the left.

F2: *Capitaine* André Dupuis; Vichy, France, 31 May 1943

A much-decorated ranker in World War I, by late 1942 Dupuis was the deputy leader of the Tunisian branch of the *Service d'Ordre Légionnaire* (SOL), the militia of the Vichy veterans' association, and was instrumental in recruiting its members to fill out the *Phalange Africaine* after the exclusion of North African trainees. After escaping from Tunisia he was promoted major, and decorated by both Vichy and Germany. He served in the LVF in Russia in 1943-44, and then in the Waffen-SS, but reportedly he chose to leave the front after the defeats in Pomerania. Photos of him being decorated as an *Officier de la Légion d'Honneur* show Dupuis wearing an unbadged *képi* apparently in the light blue and *garance*-red of the *Tirailleurs Tunisiens*. Most officers of the combat company came from the *Légion Tricolore,* and despite its now semi-defunct status Dupuis wears on his M1939 tunic LT unpiped staff collar patches. He displays on their ribbons his new Officer's Cross and Iron Cross 2nd Class and his World War I *Croix de Guerre* with citation stars and 'palms', but otherwise only ribbon bars. On his right breast pocket is the black *Phalange Africaine* shield with gold *francisque* and edging.

F3: *Volontaire, Phalange Nord-Africaine*; Dordogne, France, spring 1944

Formed in January–February 1944 by SS-Staf Helmut Knochen, deputy SIPO and SD commander in France, this unit enlisted resident North Africans for anti-Resistance service. It numbered some 300 men in five platoons, one of which served in the Dordogne until disbanded in August, by which time it had earned a murderous reputation. About six French officers led by SS-Hstuf Henri Lafont, and some 20 NCOs, all wore SD uniform. The rankers often received *Milice* garments, but this grey jacket is unidentified. A group photograph shows them all armed with 9mm Sten sub-machine guns, recovered from British supply drops to the Resistance *maquisards*.

G: FRENCH WAFFEN-SS

G1: W-Oberscharführer Henri Fenet; SS-Junkerschule Bad Tölz, December 1943

Volunteering for the French Army in 1939, in May 1940 S/Lt Fenet was wounded twice, and awarded the *Croix de Guerre*. He was released from POW camp in November 1942, soon joining the *Milice Française* and, in October 1943, the Waffen-SS. Quickly promoted to senior NCO rank, he is illustrated on his arrival at Bad Tölz for a shortened officer training course in January–March 1944. He wears the W-SS '*Schiffchen*' M1940 field cap; his greatcoat bears W-SS black shoulderstraps piped infantry-white, with the all-round NCO *Tresse* lace and single star of his rank, and the SS sleeve eagle, but neither collar patches nor a French sleeve shield. By August 1944, W-Ostuf Fenet commanded 3. Kp of the 8. SS-Frw-Sturmbrigade battle group in Galicia (Iron Cross 2nd Class); in February 1945, I/ W-Gren-Rgt 57 in Pomerania (Iron Cross 1st Class, promotion to W-Hstuf); and in April-May 1945, Sturmbataillon 'Charlemagne' in Berlin. He was wounded in the foot, but remained with his men, and on 29 April was presented with the Knight's Cross by SS-Brigaf Möhnke. In 1949 a French court sentenced him to 20 years' hard labour for collaboration, but he was released in 1959, and lived until 2002.

G2: W-Oberschütze, I/ Waffen-Grenadier-Regiment 57; Galician front, August 1944

This senior private serving within Kampfgruppe 'Schafer' wears the M1942 *Feldbluse* and M1943 trousers, canvas anklets, ankle boots, and a helmet roughly camouflaged with splashes of paint. Note that he is still equipped with the Kar 98k rifle and its belt kit. The Waffen-SS national arm-shield for French volunteers (see Plate H3) had been issued at the Neweklau training camp from March 1944. While such insignia were by regulation (15 April 1944) to be applied a finger's width below the SS eagle on the left sleeve, French volunteers initially attached it on the forearm, as if they wished to make a distinction. Strangely, the German command seem to have raised no objections to this practice. For space reasons, this man has moved the *'Blitz'* badge of a qualified signaller from the forearm to the upper sleeve.

G3: W-Rottenführer, Sturmbataillon 'Charlemagne'; Berlin, April-May 1945

Lefèvre (*Militaria* No. 119) states that this combination, of the field-grey M1942 tunic with the camouflage trousers of the so-called 'pea-pattern' SS M1944 *Drillichanzug getarnt* field uniform, was characteristic in W-Hscha Rostaing's 3. Kp (formerly 6./ SS-Btl 58); the regiment only received a partial issue of camouflage clothing on about 10 April. The field-grey M1943 'universal field cap' *(Einheitsfeldmütze)* bears a silver-grey woven SS death's-head on the front and a small SS eagle-and-swastika on the left side. The tunic collar patches bear the SS-runes on his right, and on his left the insignia of this junior NCO rank. (A divisional right collar-patch design showing a broadsword between laurel branches has been illustrated, but there is no evidence for its use.) The left sleeve – alone – displays the SS eagle above the national shield in their regulation placing, above rank chevrons. His belt with the W-SS buckle carries two triple sets of canvas magazine-pouches for his 7.92mm Sturmgewehr 44 assault rifle, issued only a couple of weeks previously to the whole regiment. Otherwise, belt equipment is probably limited to a 'breadbag', water canteen, and a Mauser 98k bayonet (unfixable to the StG 44) as an all-purpose tool/ weapon.

H: INSIGNIA & DECORATION

H1: The badge of the *Légion des Volontaires Français*, 1941. Normally seen only on posters, leaflets, etc., it was worn as a coloured metal collar badge on the tunics of LVF reinforcements leaving Versailles for the Eastern Front between April 1943 and April 1944.

H2: German Army version of French national right-sleeve patch, issued from October 1941.

H3: Waffen-SS version, worn on left sleeve, issued to different training intakes in March to July 1944.

H4: *Légion Tricolore* right-breast badge, initial embroidered version issued from late August 1942. It was also worn by some LVF personnel in France during their official subordination to the LT in that year.

H5: *Phalange Africaine* embroidered right breast badge.

H6: Divisional insignia of 33. W-Gren-Div der SS 'Charlemagne'. As marked on vehicles, notice boards, traffic signs, etc., it would normally be stencilled in black or white depending upon the background colour.

H7: The bronze *Croix de Guerre Légionnaire* (obverse), on its green-and-black striped ribbon. This was created by the *Légion Tricolore*, which officially absorbed the LVF from 22 June 1942. Instituted on 6 July 1942, and officially recognized by the Vichy goverment on 18 July, it was first awarded to LVF veterans in Paris on 27 August. A brass 'palm' on the ribbon, of which about 100 were awarded, identified citation by a senior command echelon. After the disbandment of the *Légion Tricolore* in December 1942, the Cross continued to be awarded to soldiers of the LVF.

H8: This Bevo-weave cuff title for 33. W-Gren-Div der SS 'Charlemagne' was manufactured, but there seems to be no confirmed photographic evidence for its being worn. Given the motley make-up of the formation, a story that when some were delivered the divisional commander insisted they should only be issued to men who had proved themselves in combat seems plausible. Veterans have suggested that it was worn in small numbers in the assault engineer company.

Seen here during his previous service as an SS-Sturmbannführer with 7. SS-Frw-Gebirgs-Div 'Prinz Eugen', SS-Staf Walter Zimmermann oversaw the training of the Sturmbrigade and subsequent Division 'Charlemagne' in late 1944, and was wounded soon after leading the division's Replacement Bn to join it in Pomerania in late February 1945. (US NARA)

INDEX